celebrate
every day

seeing the
extraordinary
in the
ordinary

SHAUNA
NIEQUIST

ZONDERVAN®

ZONDERVAN

Celebrate Every Day

Copyright © 2024 by Shauna Neiquist

Published in Grand Rapids, Michigan, by Zondervan. Zondervan is a registered trademark of The Zondervan Corporation, L.L.C., a wholly owned subsidiary of HarperCollins Christian Publishing, Inc.

Portions of this book were excerpted and adapted from *Cold Tangerines: Celebrating the Extraordinary Nature of Everyday Life* (9780310273608).

Requests for information should be addressed to customercare@harpercollins.com.

Zondervan titles may be purchased in bulk for educational, business, fundraising, or sales promotional use. For information, please email SpecialMarkets@Zondervan.com.

ISBN 978-1-4003-4422-2 (audio)
ISBN 978-1-4003-4420-8 (eBook)

Library of Congress Cataloging-in-Publication Data on File
ISBN 978-0-310-16786-0

Published in association with The Christopher Ferebee Agency.

Art direction: Jamie DeBruyn
Cover design: Jamie DeBruyn
Cover image: istockphoto
Interior design: Kristy Edwards

Printed in the United States of America

24 25 26 27 28 LBC 5 4 3 2 1

Introduction

It's a cool gray morning in New York, and as I write at my beloved child-sized desk-slash-nightstand, I'm looking out the window at scaffolding. New York City is obsessed with scaffolding. Put simply, scaffolding is the structure put up around a building that, for whatever reason, needs support. Maybe it's old and needs to be repaired. Or maybe it's mid-renovation. Or maybe it's new construction, and the scaffolding is less for the building and more for the safety of the people walking by, so nothing falls on them mid-construction. Scaffolding provides safety and support while a building is being transformed in some way.

Here's something I've learned the hard way: what we do every day matters far more than what we do once in a while. The daily routines and rhythms that we build to scaffold our days do more to shape who we become than the grand gestures of once-in-a-while ever could.

Especially when we're in the middle of transformation of any kind, it's the things we do every day that build a meaningful support along the way. I've had to learn, in tough seasons, how to build my own scaffolding, and one of the most important ways I do that is by reading every morning. Reading gives me a place to sort through all the wild ideas I collect in the night, and it helps give perspective and clarity for the day ahead.

My dream for this book is that it would be a grounding and clarifying way for you to begin the day. Reading and considering a few meaningful thoughts or questions is a beloved part of my morning routine, and I'd be honored if these pages became a companion in your own routine. It would bring me so much joy to think of you in your cozy quiet moments before the day starts whirling at full volume.

I began my writing life with a handful of deeply held beliefs: that our daily lives matter so deeply, that they're all we have, and that if we learn to look for beauty and divinity and magic right in our own living rooms and kitchen tables, we'll begin to see those sparks of beauty more and more often. That's what this book is about: being the kind of people who see.

What a beautiful image: all of us in all our homes—in our tiny city apartments or farmhouses or dorms, all of us choosing to begin our days with the belief that those days are worth loving, worth investing in, worth savoring, worth holding with both hands, and more than anything, worth celebrating.

What Matters Most

I believe that everyday life as it's unfolding on our plain old streets and sidewalks is the most extraordinary thing most of us will ever experience. I believe that daily life is where our lives change, where we learn to love, where we learn from our mistakes, where we sense God's presence, where we learn to tell the truth and make things right, where our hearts are broken and our wounds are laid bare and healed up. So many of the lofty concepts of faith and truth and meaning find their value and grounding not in conceptual spaces but in kitchens and living rooms and subway stations and in the silence between words and while you're folding the laundry. This is where life is. This is where everything is.

For me, it's all about daily, ordinary life. It's all about being a noticer, as a spiritual act. I notice as a way of saying thank you, as a sacrament almost, as a way of bearing witness to what's lovely and good and meaningful in the world.

I love to cook, and there are a few people in my life over the years who've been my favorite people to feed, and what I love about feeding those people is how much they notice— they eat with passion, full mouths, full plates, and they notice color and flavor and texture. They ask questions and close their eyes while they're chewing, trying to taste even more deeply. As a cook, as the person who chose the flavors, who chopped and sautéed and thought about color and texture and scent and plating, I love feeding people who notice.

I want to be a noticer. God made this world, made people, made flowers and honey and the Hudson River. The people he made with great love and in his image have written poetry and built buildings, and they perform surgery and bake bread and play the violin, and one of my most deeply held spiritual practices is noticing it all.

At the end of the day, this is what matters most to me: bearing witness to the unfolding miracle of everyday life.

Right now, notice as much as you can—what do you see? What do you smell? What are you hearing, touching, noticing around you?

Shameless Celebration

I know that the world is several versions of mad right now. I know that pessimism and grimness sometimes seem like the only responsible choices. I wake up at night and think about war and pesticides and global warming and fundamentalism and disease and crime. I worry about the world we're creating for my baby boy. I get the pessimism and the grimness.

And that's why I'm making a shameless appeal for celebration. Because I need to. I need optimism and celebration and hope in the face of violence and despair and anxiety. And because the other road is a dead end. Despair is a slow death, and a lifetime of anger is like a lifetime of hard drinking: it shows in your face and your eyes and your words even when you think it doesn't.

The only option, as I see it, is this delicate weaving of action and celebration, of intention and expectation. Let's act, read, protest, protect, picket, learn, advocate for, fight against, but let's be careful that in the midst of all that accomplishing and organizing, we don't bulldoze over a world that's teeming with beauty and hope and redemption all around us and in the meantime. Before the wars are over, before the cures are found, before the wrongs are righted, Today, humble Today, presents itself to us with all the ceremony and bling of a glittering diamond ring: *Wear me*, it says. *Wear me out. Love me, dive into me, discover me*, it pleads with us.

The discipline of celebration is changing my life, and it is because of the profound discoveries that this way of living affords me that I invite you into the same practice. Celebration is a tap dance on the fresh graves of apathy and cynicism, the creeping belief that this is all there is, and that God is no match for the wreckage of the world we live in. What God does in the tiny corners of our day-to-day lives is gorgeous and headline-making, but we have a bad habit of saving the headlines for only the scary.

There are a lot of good books about what's wrong, what's broken, what needs fixing and dismantling and deconstructing. I read them, and I hope you do too. But there might be a little voice inside of you, like there is inside of me, a voice that asks, "Is that all? Is this all there is?" And to that tiny, holy voice, I say, "No way, kiddo, there's so much more, and it's all around us, and it's right in front of our eyes."

To choose to celebrate in the world we live in right now might seem irresponsible. But I believe it is a serious undertaking, and one that has the potential to return us to our best selves, people who choose to see the best, believe the best, yearn for the best. Through that longing to be our best selves, we are changed and inspired, able to see the handwriting of a holy God where another person just sees the same old tired streets and sidewalks.

The world is alive, blinking and clicking, winking at us slyly, inviting us to get up and dance to the music that's been playing since the beginning of time, if you bend all the way down and put your ear to the ground to listen for it.

> What can you do to intentionally celebrate small things this week?

On Waiting

I have always, essentially, been waiting. Waiting to become something else, waiting to be that person I always thought I was on the verge of becoming, waiting for that life I thought I would have. In my head, I was always one step away. In high school, I was biding my time until I could become the college version of myself, the one my mind could see so clearly. In college, the post-college "adult" person was always looming in front of me, smarter, stronger, more organized. Then the married person, then the person I'd become when we have kids. For my entire life, I have waited to become the next version of myself, because that's when life will really begin.

And through all that waiting, here I am. My life is passing, day by day, and I am waiting for it to start. I am waiting for that time, that person, that event when my life will finally begin. John Lennon once said, "Life is what happens when you're busy making other plans." For me, life is what was happening while I was busy waiting for my big moment. I was ready for it and believed that the rest of my life would fade into the background, and that my big moment would carry me through life like a lifeboat.

But this is what I'm finding, in glimpses and flashes: this is it. This is it, in the best possible way. That thing I'm waiting for, that adventure, that movie-score-worthy experience unfolding gracefully. This is it. Normal, daily life ticking by on our streets and sidewalks, in our houses and apartments, in our beds and at our dinner tables, in our dreams and prayers and fights and secrets—this pedestrian life is the most precious thing any of us will ever experience.

I believe that this way of living, this focus on the present, the daily, the tangible, this intense concentration, not on the news headlines, but on the flowers growing in your own garden, the children growing in your own home, this way of living has the potential to open up the heavens, to yield a glittering handful of diamonds where a second ago there was coal. This way of living and noticing and building and crafting can crack through the movie sets and soundtracks that keep us waiting for our own life stories to begin, and set us free to observe the lives we have been creating all along without even realizing it.

I believe that if we cultivate a true attention, a deep ability to see what has been there all along, we will find worlds within us and between us, dreams and stories and memories spilling over. The nuances and shades and secrets and intimations of love and friendship and marriage and parenting are action-packed and multicolored, if you know where to look.

Today is your big moment. Moments, really. The life you've been waiting for is happening all around you. You have stories worth telling, memories worth remembering, dreams worth working toward, a body worth feeding, a soul worth tending, and beyond that, the God of the universe dwells within you. And you have been given today.

> What are some daily things in your life that you might be missing out on, waiting for that Big Moment?

Spark

I went to Westmont College, two thousand miles from my hometown. My decision to go there was partially out of heartbreak and desperation, having been rejected by my dream school, and partially out of a strange, deep feeling, a feeling I believe was God's urging.

During that season, all I could see about faith were the

things that offended me, the things I couldn't connect with. But even then, there was this tiny hope inside me, like a lighter that's almost out of juice, misfiring, catching for just a second, this tiny hope that maybe there was a way of living this faith that I just hadn't found yet.

I thought about God, even though I didn't talk about him. I didn't have big questions on the nature of the Trinity or the end of the world. Essentially, I wanted to know if there was room in the Christian world for someone like me. Because it didn't always seem like there was.

The journey back toward faith came in flashes and moments and entirely through pain. I wanted to build my life on my own terms. I felt like having faith was like having training wheels on your bike, and I wanted to ride without those training wheels even if I fell. For a while, I loved it. I felt creative and smart and courageous.

And then everything unraveled over the course of a year. I was heartbroken and confused and very much alone, and I started doing the craziest thing: I dug out my Bible. I have no idea why, really. I sat alone on my bed on a Saturday afternoon with the light slanting through my window. I was a literature major, so my room was crammed with books, and underneath a tall stack of books on the windowsill, I found my Bible. I just held it. I don't think I even read it that day. I just held it on my lap with both hands, like it was a cat.

I wanted to connect with God somehow, so I decided that I would go to the beach every night at sunset. It was the most sacred thing I could think to do. I wasn't ready yet for church, but I was ready for God, and I have always believed that the ocean is one of the surest places to find him. I started praying a little bit more honestly and listening a little bit more closely.

There was something inside me, some hopeful, small, faltering voice that said, "There's room for you." I don't know why, but I trusted that voice.

And against all odds, here I am, deeply, wholly committed to God and to his church. Looking back, I loved those years. Those years made me believe in the journey and respect it, the way you respect deep water if you've ever swum out too far and been surprised by the waves. I know what that journey can do in people. I know what it did in me, and I don't take it lightly. I have some very sobering scars and memories that I carry with me as reminders of that season. They remind me how dangerous that path is, and how beautiful.

I'm thankful for God's constant flickering and sparking flame inside me, planted in me years ago and fighting to keep burning. I know that tiny flame is the most precious thing I have, and that it can ignite a forest fire inside any heart and can burn away a lifetime of apathy and regret and distance.

Becoming Family

Aaron and I were married on a hot August night on Michigan Avenue in Chicago, near the lake and Buckingham Fountain and the Art Institute. I walked down the aisle to a Beatles song, and we danced and ate crab cakes and chocolate cake from Sweet Thang in Wicker Park, and lots of our friends sang along with the band. We watched the fireworks over Navy Pier blend in with the sizzle of the city sky. It was both sweet and a little bit wild, like the best parties are.

One of the things I said to Aaron in our wedding vows was, "When I am with you, wherever we are, I am home." It was, I thought, a beautiful and romantic thing to say, and I really felt it. Aaron has a way of settling me down and making peace in me when everything feels crazy and alien. The more time I spent with him when we first met, the stronger and more peaceful I felt, like I had eaten a delicious and nutritious breakfast.

I didn't actually think, though, that I would have to put our vows into practice quite so quickly. We met and dated in the town both our families lived in, and when we got married, we lived in that same town, near old friends and cousins and siblings. And then just a few months after our first anniversary, a friend of ours asked us to think about moving to be a part of his church, three hours away, for Aaron to be a worship leader there.

We drove up to Grand Rapids, Michigan, to talk to our friend about the church, and when we got back into the car, I started to cry, and continued crying most of the way back to Chicago. Aaron, I could see, was very excited about the prospect of the move, and very puzzled by the tears. It was an honor that they would invite him into this job. And all I could do was cry. I think I could feel, right then, the inevitability of it, that I knew somehow that we were moving, and I had already begun to mourn.

When I said to him on our wedding day that when I was with him, I was home, I did not mean, "Let's move to Michigan and see if I'm right, okay?" I meant, "I love you so much, and let's stay in Chicago where my parents and my friends are, how about that?" I had thought that we became a family the day we were married. What I have found, though, is that the web starts as just one fine filament on that day, and spins and spins around us as life presents itself to us day by day. And on some days, the strands spin around us double-time, spinning us like a top and binding us like rubber cement.

A wedding didn't make Aaron my family, or a honeymoon, or grudgingly giving him one half of the storage space in the bathroom (let's be honest—one quarter). Family gets made when the world becomes strange and disorienting, and the only face you recognize is his. Family gets made when the future obscures itself like a solar eclipse, and in the intervening darkness, you decide that no matter what happens in the night, you'll face it as one.

What big or little moments have built your sense of family?

DAY 6

Puppies

In my early twenties, I began leading a group of ten girls, quite by accident. We were short on volunteer leaders for a weekend retreat, so I said I could take a group. Somehow, it was communicated to the girls that I would be their leader forever and ever, and when they found out, they pounced on me and hugged me and jumped up and down, and in that moment, I didn't have the heart to say that I had really only agreed to love them for a few days.

We made it through that weekend, although I called them by the wrong names most of the time. About half of them had almost the same name, and they had the adolescent habit of wearing almost identical clothes. They were a blur of bright tank tops and carefully ripped jeans, and I always felt like I was in the middle of a tornado or a high-speed chase. Ten sophomore girls in one room multiply somehow, and you could swear there are a hundred of them.

We then started meeting every week. I'd prepare a discussion, and then they'd want to spend the whole time talking about tampons. I'd invite them to my house and find one of them going through my cupboards and another going through my trash. They called at all hours of the night and day and stopped over at my house and my office constantly, and apparently never had anywhere else to be after their visit. They sometimes got so excited to see me that when they hugged me, they knocked me down, even though it was never more than five days since I'd seen them last. Sometimes one of them would tell me something that was really true and important about her life. Or one of them would ask me something about life with God that really mattered to her.

Somehow they burrowed into one of the deepest parts of my life and my heart. They became something between friends and little sisters and extensions of my younger selves. They became a central part of my world, my thoughts, my prayers. My schedule became more and more wrapped around their term papers and proms and problems, and my home became more and more the safest landing spot for this group of girls.

I began to love them because they were mine, because we were us, because of the funny and sweet and strange things they did and said. They're smart and honest, and they make big mistakes and dream gorgeous bright dreams. Sometimes they tell me everything, and sometimes they try not to tell me things, but then the other girls tell me anyway.

When I think about how God made us to live, when people talk about true community, I think of them, this lovely, bizarre group of teenage girls who came over unannounced and never left when they were supposed to, who let me into their fears and their secrets, and cared about my fears and my secrets. They loved me with a force that I think only comes with youth, a wide and fierce and expressive force, and I loved them with that same love, because being with them let me live like I was young.

They uncovered something good in me and gave me all the permission in the world to love with that wide-open love, unmeasured and uncalculated, like a puppy in a box with all of her puppy-friends, right up close to them, feeling warm and safe.

Old House

I've always thought of myself as an old-house person, a person who appreciates character over perfection, who likes the bumps and bruises of an old home. So when we moved to Grand Rapids, we bought an English Tudor built in 1920 with a Hobbit-house sloping roof. I fell in love with its arched doorways and hardwood floors and funny little corners and built-in cabinets. We moved in and started fixing it up, painting, and putting in new outlets and new fixtures.

And then when I went over to a friend's brand-new house, I was overcome with jealousy, not because it was fancy or big, but because the toilets didn't run, and none of the windows were painted shut, and none of the doorknobs got stuck. When I got back to my house, all I could see were the imperfections, the things that were not yet fixed up. The uneven floors and cracked tiles and squeaky drawers. The funny-smelling basement with big pieces of the basement ceiling on the floor.

While I think of myself as an old-house girl, I guess there's still a lot of new house in me. I want to love the imperfections, but in a weak moment, I want central air and new countertops so bad I can't take it.

And it's not really about the house, is it? It's about me. I can't handle any more things that are not quite right in my life, because I feel like that's all I've got. I feel like every single part of my life has bumps and bruises and broken pieces. I want to be all shiny and new, all put together, and I just can't get there. The things I try to forget don't go away, and the mistakes I've made don't go away, and I'm a lot like my old house, cracked and mismatched and patched over.

On my worst days, I start to believe that what God wants is perfection. That God is a new-house God. That everything has to work just right, that I need to be completely fixed up. But many of the best stories in the Bible, the ones where God does sacred, magical things through people, have a cast of characters with kind of shady pasts, some serious fixer-uppers.

In my best moments, I practice believing that God loves me as-is, even if I never do get my act together. I put my hand on the plaster wall, nubbly and textured, and I think thankful thoughts about the walls. Then I put my hand on the floor, and I think thankful thoughts about the floor, even though it's scratched and ridged and you can see where one of my black heels lost its little cap and the metal part left tiny round divots in the floor. I imagine that God does that to me, puts his hand on my head, on my heart, on my savage insecurities, and as he does it, he thinks thankful thoughts about me: "I didn't ask you to become new and improved today. That wasn't the goal. You were broken down and strange yesterday, and you still are today, and the only one freaked out about it is you."

Little by little, my funny old broken-down house is teaching me that good enough is good enough. Maybe we'll take the home-improvement next step, whatever that might be, and maybe we won't, but my house will keep me warm and dry until then, and I'll try to be kind and gentle to my house and to myself in the meantime.

What messy parts of your life are you making peace with?

Island

For years, our family has been going to a tiny little island for our vacations. The island is four miles long, and there are more stray dogs and chickens than cars, and the water is the palest aqua you can imagine, dazzling and surreal. Everything is slightly damp and smells like salt and rum and french fries, and the roar of the sea against the island lulls you and makes you feel a million miles from home. We leave the windows open so the sea air can blow through the little house we stay in, and we ride around in a golf cart and keep an open tab at the grocery store, so we can just run in for a package of English ginger nut biscuits or a six-pack of Coke. There's a small shop that sells us fresh lobster if we go right when they're bringing them off the boats for the day and another shop that has gorgeous, gooey baked goods.

There are a million reasons why we love it there. It's the jumble of the waves and the sand and the goats tied to stakes in people's yards and the shimmering green-blue of the water. It's the chill in the air at night, and the way the clouded sky on the bay looks at sunset, and the mangroves and the stars that are clear and shining.

It's all those things, and something else, the something that our family becomes when we are there. We're the best version of our family there, relaxed and connected and without agenda or schedule. We have conversations that unfold lazily and resolve over days instead of minutes. We're irresponsible, and we make up plans as we go, and we've been going there long enough to have patterns just like worn spots in carpet, patterns that have become traditions, things you do without thinking, that feel familiar and meaningful. The sound of the wind and the barking dogs and the steel drums seem like our sounds, and the taste of conch fritters and rum punch and coconut bread and lobster are our tastes, the taste of vacation, the taste and smell and sound of our family.

We sleep hard because the roar of the waves on the reef keeps us sleeping like babies, and we wake up early, each finding our own spots to read and write and drink coffee before the mildness of the morning burns into the blaze of the day. We eat breakfast on the porch, the screen batted by branches and stalks in the wind, the sun glinting off the water.

We rent a boat every year, and each year it varies from slightly well-loved to downright battered. We snake through the shallow areas, holding our breath, hoping we don't bump the bottom, and we tumble over the side to snorkel when we see a school of fish or a promising reef. It's hot until the sun goes behind the clouds, and then we're all fighting over a few soggy towels because we're covered with goosebumps. When we get back, we take long, hot showers and watch movies and eat strange dinners, cobbled together out of whatever we can find at the tiny island store.

We've invested that small island with as many memories as we can make, crammed it full of love and conversations and stories and long walks and meals and boat rides. Vacations are the act of grabbing minutes and hours and days with both hands, stealing against the inevitability of time.

What are some traditions you have with your own family or close friends?

Where are you the best version of yourself?

Swimming

In the summers during college, I worked at a summer camp. It was shockingly hot and humid, like living in a hair dryer, and smelled like wisteria and swamp water and soap. All day we zigzagged from our cabins to the dining hall to the archery range to the soccer fields to the zipline to the pool, always running, letting screen doors slam with a smack.

At the end of the term, before taking their kids home, the parents came to watch them compete in a swim meet. The swim meet was the first time that they would see their kids after having been away from them for a month, which is a really long time if your kids are eight. The pool is decorated with streamers, and the sky is always blue and cloudless. The parents sit in the bleachers and start yelling and waving and taking pictures when the kids walk over, waving their tanned arms like windmills on high speed.

All the counselors have jobs for the meet, and some of us are comforters. What that means is that we're assigned to a lane, and we're wearing silly costumes, and our whole job is to cheer for whichever girl is in our lane and help her do great in the race.

For one swim meet, I was the comforter in lane five. It was a long race, several lengths, and the camper in my lane, Jessie, was getting tired. "You're doing great, Jessie," I yelled. "You can make it. Keep going." She had just left the wall on her last lap, and I could tell that she was tired and the expanse in front of her seemed way too far. She went under for a second, not like she was drowning, but like she was going to give up and turn around. "You're so close, Jessie!" I called, "You can make it!" She shook her head and then got scared and started to panic and swallowed a big gulp of water, so I jumped in and swam toward her. If she touched me, she would be disqualified, but if I stayed next to her, so she knew that I was there if she needed me, she could make it to the end. She didn't need rescuing. She just needed someone close enough to keep her from getting scared again. I swam next to her, without touching her, and as we swam, I talked to her in a quiet voice. "You're tough, Jessie. I'm right here, but you can make it." When we got to the end and she touched the wall, I pulled her out of the water, and she was so tired, floppy and teary, but the first thing she did was look up at her mom and wave.

After the meet, I was soaking wet and exhausted, still wearing a crazy wig and a soggy tutu. Jessie's mom came to find me and looked right into my eyes. "As a mom, all I wanted to do was run down the bleachers and jump in with my clothes on to finish that race with my daughter. Thank you for caring about my child the way I would have."

Maybe some of what we're doing here is representing the goodness and love of God in tangible ways. You're showing that love to the people in your life and then sometimes they're showing it to you, and when your friend isn't going to make it to the edge of the pool, you jump in with your clothes on and swim next to her.

> When has someone showed up for you in an unexpected way?

DAY 10

The Bookstore

Last year, I was at my favorite bookstore because I was feeling sort of fragile and overwhelmed, and one of the things that usually makes me feel better is a bookstore. I was looking through the cards, the ones that have quotes on the front, and they're all big, inspirational, "seize the day"-type quotes, from people like Eleanor Roosevelt and Albert Einstein. If you read them on a good day, you're like, "I will, Eleanor Roosevelt, I will change the world one tiny moment at a time!" But on kind of a cranky, bad day, you read them, and you think, "Well, that's why you people are famous, because you do wonderful inspirational things, and all I do is try to get through the day without crying or losing my mind." So I was looking at all these cards, and usually I'm just a sucker for them, but on that night, I felt worn out and hollow. I looked at this whole big wall of cards, and each one was making me feel more broken down and scraped away inside, so far from inspiration and hope. Then I saw one in the corner, in black and white, and it said, "You too? I thought I was the only one."

And it hit something inside me, and in the card aisle at Schuler's, I started to cry. Really cry, like the kind of tears that have been waiting to come out for a long time. That night I didn't need big, great, beautiful words from important people. I just needed to know that I wasn't alone. "You too? I thought I was the only one."

True friendship is a sacred, important thing, and it happens when we drop down into that deeper level of who we are, when we cross over into the broken, fragile parts of ourselves. We have to give something up in order to get friendship like that. We have to give up our need to be perceived as perfect. We have to give up our ability to control what people think of us. We have to overcome the fear that when they see the depths of who we are, they'll leave. But what we give up is nothing in comparison to what this kind of friendship gives to us. Friendship is about risk. Love is about risk. If we can control it and manage it and manufacture it, then it's something else, but if it's really love, really friendship, it's a little scary around the edges.

Friendship is acting out God's love for people in tangible ways. We were made to represent the love of God in each other's lives, so that each person we walk through life with has a more profound sense of God's love for them. Friendship is an opportunity to act on God's behalf in the lives of the people that we're close to, reminding each other who God is. When we do the hard, intimate work of friendship, we bring a little more of the divine into daily life. We get to remind one another about the bigger, more beautiful picture that we can't always see from where we are.

When have you experienced comfort knowing that you weren't alone?

The Key

My friend Annette and I met our freshman year in college. She was funny and fun, just as she is now, and she was the real thing, a strong, intuitive, wise person whose words carried serious weight with me, just as they do now. She drove a red Wrangler and seemed to me to be the quintessential California girl. I was certainly the quintessential Midwestern girl in her eyes. She mocked the way I said "maaahm" for "mom" and laughed at my modest one-piece swimsuit.

We became breakfast regulars at the Summerland Beach Café. The first time we went there, I had a gooey cinnamon roll and about two gallons of black coffee, and she ordered the Ranchhand Breakfast, or some such thing, pancakes and eggs and potatoes and bacon. It was enough food for three men, and it cracked me up to see this tiny blonde put away so much food. We routinely went swimming at Cabrillo Beach instead of going to our science class, and we routinely set out to go running and ended up stopping off for margaritas at the beach, or free iced coffees at Starbucks, begged from her friend Javier who worked there.

We always said that we wanted to live in the same town, but she got married and lived in the town she grew up in, and then I got married and lived in the town I grew up in. Then against all odds, she and her husband moved from San Diego to Grand Rapids, partially for a job, partially for a church, and partially because we never stopped talking about what it would be like to really get to be best friends, everyday friends, the kind of friends we can't be when all we have are weekend visits and emails.

The day after Easter, they arrived at our house, Annette and her husband, Andrew, and their ninety-five-pound dog, Sydney, and a strange assortment of things, including a large bag of tea and an extremely large bag of spices. Apparently, Annette's mother advised them that moving is costly enough without having all your tea and spices stuck in storage for months and having to buy all new ones. So they each had about two pairs of pants, but all the coriander and Earl Grey they needed.

While they looked for a house, they lived with us. For two months, the four of us and the dog tripped over each other and laughed and told stories and talked about how terrible and hard it is to move. The day they moved into their new house, they left before we were up, and when I went downstairs there was a card from them. When I opened the card, a key slid out, and I started to cry, because this thing, this special, crazy season was over, and they were giving back our key. I thought about how warm and fun and odd our little household was, the four of us trying to make dinner, and talking about old things and new things, and laughing about how messy it was with all of us there. And then I read the card, and it wasn't our house key. It was their new house key. The card said, "You are as much a part of our home as we have been a part of yours."

Nobody would ever recommend having your college roommate and her husband and their dog move across the country and live in your house for two months. But that's that thing, that rare, beautiful thing. Annette shows me over and over that the closer you get to someone, the more that friendship gives you and the more force and power it has to make your life bigger and richer.

What are a few ways friendship has made your life bigger and richer?

DAY 12

Paris

One of the best things my dad ever said was that he never wanted school to get in the way of my education. What it meant was that, among other things, he thought thirteen was definitely old enough to travel alone. I had been traveling with him for years, and when I did, he made sure that I learned, little by little, how to untangle myself from the snags of international travel. Sometimes he would have me check us in, so that I knew how, or figure out which train to take, or who to ask about a hotel. Sometimes he would tell me after a situation had unfolded how to yield better results next time.

The week after I finished eighth grade, I boarded a plane by myself and flew from Chicago to Cincinnati to LaGuardia to Frankfurt to Charles de Gaulle in Paris. I felt so grown up as I rehearsed my French phrases and gripped my little case with my passport and credit card and tickets like they were my best friends. When I arrived at Charles de Gaulle, I found my rolling suitcase and the map I had marked and walked across the bridges toward the apartment where I would stay. My parents had a friend who agreed to let me stay with her for a week. What we hadn't really discussed before I left was the fact that in exchange for rent, she answered the phones in her building all day, so, really, if there was anything I wanted to see in Paris, I was going to have to find it alone.

So I did. Every morning she brought me *chocolat chaud* and a bit of a baguette, and we spread out the map on the floor and made lists of all the places I wanted to see. All day I tromped around, on the metro and on the bus and over the bridges, to the Musee D'Orsay and the Place des Invalides and the Centre Pompidou. I ate crepes with Nutella for every meal because I was thirteen. I walked the tall steps at Montmartre and Sacré Cœur and wandered by the street artists and vendors there, rehearsing my phrases furiously several times before I blurted them out all in one breath—"I like your painting!" or "What a pretty dog!"

I know I was happy before that, that there were things that made me happy, but there was something that happened to me on that trip. It began a love affair with traveling alone. I felt so small and so anonymous, surrounded by the sounds and smells and sights of a place I'd only read about, and I could go as quickly or as slowly as I wanted to. There are only two things I like to do alone: reading and traveling, and for the same reason. When you travel, and when you read, you are not actually alone, but rather surrounded by other worlds entirely, the footsteps and phrases of whole other lives keeping you company as you go.

I love the perfect happiness of being alone in a magical place, like something great is always about to happen to you. And it always is. There's always some side street or café or painting in a gallery or park or person or something that takes your breath away. And you look differently when you're alone. When you're with someone else, you share each discovery, but when you are alone, you have to carry each experience with you like a secret, something you have to write on your heart.

> What have you learned about yourself after spending some time alone?

These Are the Days

When I was twenty, I spent a semester traveling through England, Ireland, and Scotland with other English and theater majors, seeing lots of live theater, reading Hardy in Hardy Country and Austen in her hometown and so on. It was as strange and fantastic as it sounds, complete with extremely quirky thespians, obscure-poetry-quoting literati, and innumerable hours on a coach.

Before the semester abroad, I knew a few of them from classes, friends of friends, acquaintances, but over the course of the trip, six of us became a little family. We became a tight little band of troublemakers, brothers and sisters, witnesses to several months of stories that our friends at home would never believe if we told them.

We began in Edinburgh, still one of my favorite cities. We went to shows at all hours of the night and day, and our homebase was Hengrave Hall, a sprawling fifteenth-century manor house in the middle of absolutely nowhere.

It was gorgeous and damp and seemed like the kind of place that would be haunted. For breakfast, we had gallons of tea, heavily sugared, and stacks of toast, and for lunch, something British-y—and by that, I mean warm, mushy, and salty—with dessert, a cake or crumble over which we poured warm custard. Lots and lots of warm custard.

Living at Hengrave was sort of like living in a British novel and sort of like being sick. Because we were there for stretches of several days at a time, and the nearest town was several miles away, we padded around in slippers and sweatshirts clutching novels and cups of tea, like well-read invalids.

On warmer days, we explored the grounds, the orchards, the gardens, and the tiny stone chapel, and on nights when we stayed out so late that they locked the doors, and our roommates didn't respond to the rocks we threw at their windows, we slept in the unheated summerhouse and sneaked back into the main house in the morning. We memorized long passages of Shakespeare while perched on radiators because of the chill, and some of us learned to knit, dragging around balls of yarn like lifeless cats.

One of the reasons I went on the trip was that my favorite professor was teaching the semester course. She was beautiful and strong and tall with blonde hair, and she wore several thin gold rings on one finger. She pushed me, as a writer and as a person of faith and as a woman. There were times when I failed her, and when I did, her disappointment crushed me, and then her grace healed me.

On the first day of the trip, in Edinburgh, this was her prayer: "Help us to be brave with one another, for these are the days." She was right. They were the days. They were singularly beautiful, terrible days. In some ways, I was never more myself, and in others, never more unrecognizable. But we were brave with one another, which is, I'm finding, more than one can ask for. She was brave with me, telling me the truth about myself, and I think I was a little bit brave with her, withstanding her disappointment and letting it reach down to the deepest parts of me and draw me up to a better self.

When have you been brave with someone? What has that taught you about yourself?

DAY 14

Visions and Secrets

When I think about my child-self, my little girl memories, all that little girl wanted to be was a storyteller, a poet, a person who gathers and arranges words like some people gather and arrange flowers. Words are the breakdown through which I see all of life, instead of molecules or notes or chords or colors. Words in even black and white snakes, back and forth across the page, the portals through which a little girl found a big world, and through which, now, a grown-up girl is trying to pass.

When I write, I can see things that I can't otherwise see, and I can feel things that I can't otherwise feel. Things make sense, in flashes and glimpses, in me and around me. They unravel themselves and line up into black and white rows, and those rows nourish me, sliding down my throat like noodles.

I can feel things turning, slowly. I can feel this tiny, fragile writer person getting bigger, like a candle flame growing. Tonight is a writing night, and I feel giddy, antsy, bold in a new way. I feel like I have a secret: I am becoming something else. On the outside, I look like a person who has a desk and meetings, but underneath, I'm a writer.

I am stunned, still, and keep marveling at it. A little bit ago, things were murky, tangled, and teary. I knew that something in me was changing, but it felt vague and not-yet-here, like a low train whistle or a growl of thunder in the distance. I've spent a hundred nights trying to find words for what's happening, feeling something strange and new being born.

For me, to write is an act of rebellion, an uprising

against that part of me that needs to be responsible, helpful, adaptive. It is one of the first things, maybe the very first thing, that is entirely my own, that doesn't help anyone, doesn't make anyone else's life easier, doesn't facilitate or provide structure or administrative support for anyone else. I've always been a team player, a utility player, a workhorse, and to do something sheerly out of a deep love for the act itself feels foreign and vaguely scandalous. It feels, I'm realizing, selfish.

I feel, in the best moments, in spite of the uncertainty, in spite of the fear, like Lily Briscoe in *To the Lighthouse. Yes, she thought, laying down her brush in extreme fatigue, I have had my vision.* I had that line written on my wall for years, years ago, and now it holds a whole new richness. I have had my vision, and I thought it would come in a flash, a bright beam of knowing. But it has come in the same way that all things come to me. It has come to me with a fight. It has come to me the hard way, through tears and fog and fear and chaos, and now has landed in the palm of my hand like a firefly. There now, I have had my vision.

What is something you've always wanted to do but never thought it was possible?

Stuck

When I write, about half an hour breezes by usually, and then it all screeches to a halt like cars crashing. I get stuck, convinced it was a bad idea to even start. My therapist once told me to start where you're stuck. I get stuck because I try to map out every dip and turn, try to write an ending, literally and figuratively, before a beginning even exists. So I don't write, but with the energy that I could use on writing, I worry instead. There is a blanket of depression and anxiety and frustration covering over everything, and I blame anything within striking distance.

After I'm through ranting and raving, I realize tragically that I still feel the sadness and terror, and that I did not, in fact, solve my problem. It's the fear and the chaos and the strange and wonderful and entirely new thing unfolding in me. I kept finding myself in tears, hoping for a life that was wholly different from the one I was living. I couldn't figure out if I was just tired and needed a vacation, or if I was scared and needed to quit.

But sometimes I sit in silence, waiting for something, hoping for something to break through, crack through, and connect the dots that felt scattered all over my life. I prayed a lot in the middle of the night, prayers that sounded more like sobs, not at all sure what I was even asking for.

But little by little, when I start where I'm stuck, over and over and over, getting stuck and unstuck, something cracks through, and life reveals itself to me like a scroll unfurling, and I write about it. I struggle against myself, and I write about it. I feel afraid, and I write about it. I don't figure out the solution in any tidy way, and I don't have a sharp and clever revelation, but bit by bit, writing is starting to worm its way into the dailiness of my life and is creating a home there. It is becoming less and less of a strange distant dream and more and more of the actual way I live.

> How do you set yourself free when you've been stuck in a pattern you've created for yourself?

DAY 16

Babymaking

Aaron and I had decided in the fall that after we went on a trip in November, it would be baby-making time. We had been married for four years, were about to turn thirty, and had done all of those things we said we wanted to do before we had kids. We were extremely and satisfyingly irresponsible.

One morning in January, when the alarm went off, I took a pregnancy test and climbed back in bed with Aaron to wait. "Pregnant," it said. Distinctly, plainly. I showed it to Aaron, who became wide awake very quickly. It seems like there would be so many things to say in that moment, but Aaron and I found ourselves silenced under the enormity and shock of it. We laid side by side in bed, staring at the ceiling, amazed and afraid.

I didn't expect that right from the beginning, the baby would occupy so much of my mind and spirit. I knew it would occupy my body, but I was surprised by how deeply it took root in my thoughts and prayers and dreams. I was never unaware of it. I never forgot about it, never woke up surprised by my big belly. It is much more an active thing than I thought, a thing to do, to care for, to think about. I thought it happened to you, and then at some point a baby came and that's when the life change began. But that's not the case at all.

In some ways, it's just waiting. Waiting and preparing. But in other ways, it feels like having a secret all your own, something precious to carry around with you, like knowing about a surprise party no one else knows about, like having a tiny friend with you all the time.

I can't wait to meet this little person, to see his eyes and his face, to see whose face we see in his, Aaron's or my dad's or my brother's. I can't wait to tell him about all the things we did together when I was pregnant, about going to Zurich and Orlando and Harbor Springs and Chicago, about how much we started loving him the moment he existed, and how much he has changed our lives even now. About how I walked around and around the neighborhood, thinking about the nursery, rubbing my belly, trying to tell him that we will take care of him the very best we can.

I don't know what the future holds. I don't know what I'll do and what I won't do in my life. But I can tell already that baby making is going to be one of the very best things I do. And Henry-making is my proudest accomplishment yet.

> What's something you're excited about in the future?
> What occupies the space in your mind?

DAY 17

The Red Tree

A few months ago, in the golden crackle of fall, I woke up early on a Friday morning. I was getting a cold. That month, we hosted a baby shower, a wedding shower, and a rehearsal dinner at our house. I made a job transition at the church, which we all know means you work two entire jobs for a while and call it a transition. A good friend got married, another celebrated her thirtieth birthday, another found out she's pregnant, and another adopted a newborn. My husband had his wisdom teeth removed, because we had so much extra time that month for elective surgery, and on this particular Friday morning, I was two weeks from teaching at an event, and had no idea what I was going to say, or what I was going to wear, both of which were causing me just a teeny bit of stress.

My husband needed more gauze for his teeth, and more ice cream, and more soup, and while I was going, more strawberries. Okay.

I threw a coat over my pajamas, flew out the door, and raced through the store, throwing things in the cart. On the way home, I had a phone conversation that totally stressed me out about one of the upcoming events. When I got home, my husband told me that I bought the wrong gauze. You would think I could get the right gauze because I had already bought it seven times that week, but it was indeed the wrong gauze.

I didn't even let him finish what he was saying. I stomped out the door, back into the car, still in my pajamas, and as I opened the garage door again, I stopped in my tracks. In the park across the street, one of the tallest trees, twice as high as a two-story house, was the brightest, most insane, lit-from-within red I have ever seen. And it took my breath away, for two reasons.

First, because it was so beyond beautiful, and second, because I had not noticed one step of its turning. I had been in and out of my driveway a zillion times in the last two weeks and could not have told you if the tree was even still standing or not. As I stood there in the driveway, I realized that I had stopped seeing the most important things to see.

I saw the to-do list, the accumulation of things in the house that would have to be shoved in closets for the parties. I saw the stack of half-finished ramblings and Post-Its all over my desk that were not turning themselves into a brilliant talk like I hoped they would. I saw the pile of things to go to the dry cleaner and the pile of work to be done and the pile of promises I had made and couldn't possibly keep.

I saw the long list of meetings and projects at work and the long list of phone calls to return. I had gifts to buy and flights to schedule and oil to change and people to celebrate. But I wasn't seeing the people or the celebrations. I wasn't seeing anything beyond the chaos of my life and my home and my calendar.

What looks like a plain old city street is just that until you lift up your eyes and see the red tree, and then you realize that this is no plain city street. This is a masterpiece just here for the week, our very own wonder of the world, and I just about missed it.

> What have you almost missed because you were too busy?
>
> What can you do to slow down and embrace the world and people around you in a more intentional way?

Exodus

Last winter, I did a study on Exodus. Not the kind of Bible study I'm used to, because I usually do the kind where a bunch of friends meet at someone's house or a coffee shop and occasionally, we do the actual study but mostly we talk and tell stories and pray at the end. This was the other kind, the kind where you have to have a really big commentary book.

I sat at a long table, surrounded by people who, apparently, actually attended the Old Testament classes at their colleges, and several of whom even went back for a second helping at various seminaries. Even though I didn't, I found myself very connected to the story of Exodus. It's a great story, a big, sweeping story about the sea and the desert and the sky, but it's also a story of incredibly fine detail, like a Fabergé egg, like a large painting with teeny tiny brush-strokes. And as much as it's a very important story, about big themes and pervasive truths about the nature of God and his people, a finely wrought web of ideas and ideals, it's also about blood and bones and midwives and frogs and fires and bread.

Exodus, and the Bible as a whole for that matter, usually comes sanitized and shrink-wrapped, like chicken breasts at the grocery store in their flat, tidy little plastic packages. But when I read it this time, it seemed a lot more like a bunch of chickens in somebody's backyard, kicking up dust, squawking and screeching and pecking each other, with red and black and white feathers glinting in the hot sun. It's less like the commentary book, with its footnotes and indices, and more like a crime novel or a gothic tale of love and belief and betrayal, a story about family and fear and animals and anger.

On the mornings that we studied Exodus, I felt myself walk through the rest of the day differently. I felt like my life, my actual daily, water and wine and blood and guts life, was a little ennobled, like I could stand up a little straighter. I ate my hummus and bread and olives at lunch, feeling like

I was a part of something old and elemental, like eating good food, fresh food made by someone's hands, was something important. It made me think about the yarn of my scarf, and how someone made it with their hands, and how threads and garments and colors mattered so much when they built the ark of the covenant.

It made me feel like even though a million things are different in my life than they were then, like email and Gore-Tex and dishwashers, some things are not so different, like bugs and yeast and the impulse to worship. There's still a big story, disguised as just regular life, and the big story is about love and death and God, and about bread and wine and olives, about forgiveness and hunger and freedom, about all the things we dream about, and all the things we handle and hold. Exodus was the Wild West, lawless and risky, and it's the cities we live in, bursting with life and meaning, and someday, when the future brings a world we can't even imagine now, Exodus will be there, in the songs and sounds and in the flesh and bones of a people who still wander and still yearn for home.

What are some elements of the big story that you notice in your own life?

Feeding People

Two of my favorite things are reading about food and watching TV shows about food. I drill my friends about what they order at restaurants and what they make for dinner. I bore my husband to tears with long descriptions of what I'm cooking for an upcoming dinner party and precisely what led me to each decision.

Feeding the people I love is a hands-on way of loving them. When you nourish and sustain someone, essentially, you're saying that you want them to thrive, to be happy and healthy and able to live well. It might matter to me because so much of the work I've done, both at church and as a writer, has taken place in my mind and in my heart, but not usually in my flesh and fingers. After a long day of writing or a long week of meetings, it returns me to myself to shop for food, to wander through the produce section, to wash and chop vegetables, to heat garlic and broth, to taste the sharpness of cheddar on whole grain bread.

So much of modern life and theology insists that what matters is my mind, my soul, my inner self, my heart, there is still this nagging part of me that knows on some deep level that the things we see and touch and hear and taste are spiritual too.

Brothers and Sisters

The idea for our housechurch began as a weekly dinner and discussion and has woven itself into phone calls and vacations and borrowed lawnmowers and weekends at the lake and last-minute babysitting. Most of our extended families live out of town, and we've wormed our way into the family places in one another's lives, into the daily intimacies of homes and heartbreaks and hard conversations. We cry together and pray together and tell each other our secrets, and I think each one of us is surprised at what we've become in one another's lives.

On the day I resigned from my job, our housechurch met, and I told them what happened. I don't remember, really, what I told them, since it was so strange and fresh. I cried a little, but not as much as I would in the weeks to come. Annette's face, furthest away from me, was shocked and angry and protective. She was measured with her words, but I could see that she was upset, and that meant something to me. They asked questions and prayed for me at the end of the night, and in that house, I felt like I wasn't alone.

Two weeks later, we met at our house. I made home-made macaroni and cheese and roasted vegetables, and after dinner, as we sat in the living room, they asked me how I was doing. I was barely comprehensible, running from one fear to the next to the next, and I kept trying to change the subject, aware that I was out of control, and also that although this was the center of the universe to me, they must have been tired of hearing about it at that point. I felt embarrassed about not being able to move forward more quickly, and about being such a wreck, and about the tears that were all over my face and neck as I spoke. But every time I thanked them for listening and tried to turn the conversation, they turned it back and spoke to me like people who love me, because, I'm realizing, they are.

At one point, one of my friends interrupted me. "You can feel however you want to feel right now. Except one thing. I keep hearing you say that you're embarrassed. I want you to stop saying that. You can feel angry, betrayed, whatever. But I don't think you have anything to be embarrassed about. And I'll never be embarrassed to be your friend."

I felt like I had been ground to dust, and those words started to put me back together. During a time when I had nothing to give but venom and tears, when I monopolized, this small circle of people were the words and fragrance and presence of God in unmistakable ways. I have never been so clingy and strange, so unmoored and lacking in appropriate small talk, and I am beyond thankful to my friends for sticking around in the worst of it.

In the moments that I thought would be the loneliest, I didn't feel lonely. I had that little band of brothers and sisters everywhere I turned, calling me, emailing me, writing me letters, taking me out for breakfast, and sitting on the porch with me, telling me the truth as they saw it, which was a lot more beautiful than the truth as I saw it then.

> When did your friends show up for you? How do you show up for your friends?

DAY 21

Enough

Two months after I left my job at a church, I spoke at a conference. I was glad, conceptually, that I had a few speaking and consulting things on the calendar. I enjoy the work, and it helped me feel like I was earning some money for our family. But at the same time, I felt so deeply vulnerable. The last thing I wanted to do was stand up in front of anyone.

What if someone asked me how things were going at my church? Did I have the right to say anything at all?

On the first morning of the event, I drove out to hear the other speakers. I didn't have to speak until the next day, but I wanted to go the first day to see what it was like. I had written my talk already—well, sort of.

On the way out there, I started feeling anxious. By the time I got to the parking lot, I was sobbing, so I stayed in the car to try to figure it out, and to try to fix my makeup. I felt illegitimate. I felt like I had no right to speak at this conference anymore. My bio in the program had been printed when I was still working at the church, and now I felt like a liar, like a poser who was clinging to something that wasn't true anymore. I slumped down in the driver's seat and laid my head back and cried and cried, until I felt hollowed out and exhausted. I went in and stood at the back of the room for a few sessions, and then I went back home and rewrote every word of my talk.

The next morning, I was scheduled to speak after the producer of X-Men and before the man who engineered the Hummer. I walked out onto the stage and said, "I'm going to tell you right now that you are not going to like what I have to say. But at this point, I have nothing left to lose, so I'm just going to tell you what I think."

And I did. I told them some of the things my friends and I had learned while we worked at churches. I told them the lessons we learned the hard way, and the things I wish I had known when I began. It wasn't clever or polished. There were no slides or video clips or touching anecdotes, but it was the best talk I have ever given, because I had nothing left to lose. I had given up on impressing them and figured that at the very least, I could give them a helpful thought for the car ride home. I didn't design a bestselling vehicle or produce a blockbuster movie, but I had spent almost a decade creating services in churches, and I told the truth as I see it about that work, about its value and its challenges.

And when the talk was over, I felt free. What I found standing on that stage is that, to my great surprise, I had my stories, my own experiences and mistakes and successes, and that those are things you don't give back when you turn in your keys and your laptop. I had never felt more alone and vulnerable, walking out onto that stage, but when I walked off, I felt just exactly like myself. I didn't represent anyone or anything. I just took up my own space and told my own stories, stories that I earned along the way. And that was enough.

How do you get through the feeling of being an imposter or unqualified to do something?

A Funeral and a Wedding

Early on a Tuesday morning in May, my brother, Todd, called me. Our friend Clark had been in an accident the night before, he told me, and he had been killed. I was on my way to the work but kept driving to South Haven, where Clark lived, where my mom was, where Todd was going to meet us. When he drove up and got out of the truck, he hugged me so hard and for so long that I thought he might knock me down, that I might bend under the weight of his grief. For the next several days, we told stories and cried and cried.

The whole town stopped, because Clark was an extraordinary person, the fourth of five boys in an extraordinary family. On the day of the visitation, literally every flower in town was at the funeral home. The florists had no more flowers, and that felt fitting, that every fragile, beautiful living thing in town wanted to be where Clark was.

Clark's funeral was on a Friday, a cool blue-sky Friday, and straight from the funeral, I flew to Chicago, because one of my oldest and dearest friends was getting married and asked me to officiate the ceremony. I felt the two events gain clarity from one another, and I was strikingly aware of the connections between them.

When I joined the families, I felt urgent and purposed. I wanted to hold them by the shoulders and whisper to them, "This is a good thing that you're doing, making a new family, joining together in love, promising to walk through life together. Because I saw something this week that I pray you will never experience, but if you do, may God bless you with a family like Clark's family. May God give you brothers to stand with, or a wife's hand to hold, or a sister to weep with, because we won't make it through these things alone. We can't stand in the way of death, but when it comes, we can stand in its face together, and celebrate life and celebrate family and celebrate having loved fiercely and expressively."

I invited them all to celebrate this new family, because a new family makes the world better. It brings people together, creates new connections, creates bonds that we all need in daily ways, and then desperately, when death comes to our home the way it did to Clark's home. It felt like a deep honor to pronounce them husband and wife, a hopeful and delicate moment rising from a week of despair.

As they danced that night, with such happiness and abandon and sweetness, I sat at the edge of the dance floor with my brother, and we both knew that the other was thinking of Clark, and who Clark might have married, and what Todd's wedding day will be like without Clark standing with him, and I thought I might burst at that moment, so full of sadness and beauty, so thrilled for this new family, this new symbol of possibility and life, and so heavy with the grief I carried with me. And that moment felt like a rare gift, like the essence of life and love and family was sitting in my hand, like a tiny bird.

> When have you been in a space between heavy grief and impossible beauty?

DAY 23

Mothers and Sons

My mom and I spent a week in Chicago this summer taking a class at a Catholic graduate school in the city. It was hot and windy, and the class was long. I was pregnant, and we were both exhausted. Every day, when the class was finished, we went straight back to the hotel and laid on our beds trying to decide whether or not to go back the next day.

On Tuesday morning of that week, while we ate pancakes at a restaurant by our hotel, my dad called from South Haven to tell us that my brother had been in a bad car accident. I could see my mom's face but couldn't hear my dad's words. When I heard her ask, "How bad is he?" I felt sick, like the lights in the restaurant were too bright and too hot or like I had swallowed a big piece of my plate thinking it was pancake. I wanted to scream at the man beside us yammering away about the window replacement business. My mom gave me the quick thumbs-up that he was fine, while she nodded, listening to Dad on the other end of the phone, but I still wanted the window man to shut it, so I could concentrate. Todd called a few minutes later to tell us that he was fine, and we felt blessed and lucky and a little bit like it wasn't real, because he sounded so fine on the phone.

After our class, though, back at the hotel, we talked to Dad again, and he told us a little more clearly how bad the accident had been, and how different it would have been if the cars had been a second earlier or later in the intersection. We started to understand that it was more than a lucky break, and that he could have died that morning, and that this was not a near miss but a miracle. We tried not to think about Clark's accident, in the same town, on an early summer morning just like that one.

All at once, my mom began to cry. She cried and cried for her son, for what could have happened, for being far away from him. She came and sat next to me on my bed, and we both put our hands on my belly, on my son. We sat there for a long time, she thinking about her big, grown son, and me thinking about my tiny son, curled up inside me. I realized in that moment how terrifying it is to be a parent, that someday, a few days before Henry's twenty-seventh birthday, someone could run a red light early in the morning, and there will be nothing in the world that I can do about it. That thought makes me unable to breathe.

I know, cognitively, that all of parenting is an effort to give your kids the ability to live without you, beyond you. But that night, on that bed, feeling so far away from my brother, my mother's son, sitting together with her, with our hands on my tiny son in my belly, I felt one of the first splitting aches that must be motherhood. I felt powerful and powerless in the same instant.

As I watch my mother, I see the size of her love for him, bigger than the ocean, beyond words and logic and sense. And I feel it too for my son, its inevitability and its enormity.

How does unconditional love affect how you feel for someone?

The Cat's Pajamas

Aaron's mom called last week that week to tell us that Grandpa Niequist, my husband's grandpa, had a heart attack. He died surrounded by his family, telling stories and singing to him. He was two months shy of his eightieth birthday.

I tried to work but couldn't. I felt powerless against the body and time and medicine, and I wished that the sheer force of my love could reverse it all. A knot of anxiety twisted like a knife, around and around and around, and in that moment the world seemed so fragile and life so dangerous and risky, and more than I could hold inside my heart and my mind.

When I first met Grandpa, he took Aaron and me fishing in the Florida Keys. We left early in the morning, with sandwiches that Grandma packed for us. Grandpa took us out to his best fishing hole, near the bridge over to the next key, and we cast out into the bright water over and over for hours. Grandpa took my fish off the hook for me, but he made me reach into the bucket myself to grab a live shrimp for bait, even though it took me several tries each time, and even though I yelped every time I plunged my hand into all the squirmy, wriggling shrimp. He loved that I was a boater, that I could tie a decent knot and knew port from starboard. At the end of the day, he told Aaron that he thought I was the cat's pajamas.

When we received the phone call, we went back to Chicago for the weekend and spent hours and hours talking about Grandpa, about his life, and about what it was like to be a part of his family. Yesterday at the funeral, at the end of the eulogy, which was beautiful and was the story of a life very well lived, the pastor talked about Grandpa's love for his family, and his sons told stories about fishing trips and family holidays and memories of the house he built for his young family and lived in until he died.

The day of his heart attack, Grandpa was trimming trees with a chainsaw. My father-in-law always said that Grandpa would die with his boots on, and I know that he meant it figuratively, but it happened literally. Grandpa spent his last wakeful moments working in the backyard near the pond where he taught his children and grandchildren to swim.

Each of us who knew him well have story after story of ways that he loved us and made us feel important. His life had an epic quality to it; a quintessentially American sense; a nostalgic, charmed quality; a story of family and music and Sundays in the backyard pond with the grandkids.

If you were to ask his children and grandchildren about him, they would tell you the things he taught them—that family comes before business, that hard work matters, that faith is the most important thing. They would not tell you he was perfect, but they would tell you that because of him, because of his role in each of their lives, they are better people, better fathers and mothers, better husbands and wives, better doctors and business owners, better church members, and better followers of Jesus.

We left the funeral tired and sad, but proud—proud to have been his children and grandchildren, proud to have been bit players in such an extraordinary story. He was the cat's pajamas.

Tell us about someone who has a lasting legacy in your life.

DAY 25

Pennies

When I was in college, people kind of stopped using pennies. The loss seemed tragic to me, so I started collecting them, in a pale blue bowl. And like with anything you're looking for, or anything you collect, the more aware you are of them, the more you see.

I started to see pennies everywhere—in the backs of

drawers, under the couch cushions, at the sticky bottom of the center console of cars. I don't know what I will do with them, but there is something satisfying about watching their numbers grow, a little army of copper coins. It feels to me that if these worthless little coins have a place, then they have a meaning. And then if I have a place, I have meaning.

So now I'm amassing pennies like you wouldn't believe. Maybe someday I will melt them all down and make a trophy. Maybe I will grout them into my bathroom tile. Maybe I will make jewelry with them. I don't know yet. But when I walk by the blue bowl in the kitchen, I find myself absently running my fingers through the coins, sure for the moment that there are things that are real and understandable, and therefore good, things I can hold on to when my hands feel empty.

My friend goes to a spiritual director, and I was asking her about it, and she said, basically, Sister Carmen asks her to talk about her life, and she points out the presence and action and grace of God when my friend didn't even notice it was there. So it was there all along, and the trick is learning to see it.

Each one of our lives is shot through, threaded in and out with God's provision, his grace, his protection, but on the average day, we notice it about as much as we really notice gravity. So what I'm trying to do is learn to see the way Sister Carmen sees. Because once you start seeing the faithfulness and the hope, you see it everywhere, like pennies. And little by little, here and there, you realize that all of life is littered with bright copper coins, that all of life is woven with bits and stories of God's goodness.

When I look back now, with these new eyes, it's like there's a bright copper path I was walking on and didn't even know it. And it's the handful of pennies that I'm clutching in my sweaty hand that gives me the faith and the strength to move forward. What gives me hope is the belief that God will be faithful, because he has been faithful before, to me and the people around me. I need the reminders. Just because I have forgotten how to see doesn't mean it isn't there. His goodness is there. His promises have been kept. All I need to do is see.

So when I'm on the edge, peering over into the unknown, trembling and terrified to move forward, devastatingly afraid to take that next step, I practice believing that full life is beyond the fear. I know that God's voice has led me to this exact place, and I grab a few pennies. They are sacred reminders that God is leading my life, and that he is saying to me, as he has been saying to his people throughout history, I will never leave you, and I've left reminders all around, if you have the eyes to see them.

What has been a reminder of God's faithfulness in your life?

Hide and Seek

About 90 percent of the reason I write is for what it does on the inside of my life, and about 10 percent for what it produces on paper. When I write, I believe the risky thought that all the ideas might have a place, instead of just running themselves around and around in a circle. Writing gives me a place to use all the flashes and thoughts and rabbit trails that rattle around in my head. Writing is my best chance at happiness, and it is the riskiest thing I can do. But that's how life is. The riskiest things always yield the best, most beautiful things.

What writing teaches me, over and over, is that God is waiting to be found everywhere, in the darkest corners of our lives, and in the simplest, lightest, most singular and luminous moments. He's hiding, like a child, in quite obvious and visible places, because he wants to be found. The miracle is that he dwells in both. I knew he dwelt in the latter, the bright and beautiful, because I had been finding him there for years, in the small moments of beauty and hope that poke through the darkness of our days.

But lately I have been finding him right within the blackness and deadness of these days. I have found a strange beauty in the darkness, one I've never seen, a slower, subtler beauty, like how a storm can make you feel more deep emotion than a sunny day ever did. When I write, I find a whole new universe I never saw before, like being underwater for the first time, having never before seen what's under the glassy surface.

Sometimes when I'm writing, if I try really hard, I can move more slowly, like a dancer or a mime, and taste things more vividly, and see not just the trees and the grass, but the individual leaves and blades. Things are richer and brighter than I thought, now that I have slowed down enough to see them. I can see that for years I have been wanting to live this way, and at the same time have been very afraid of what I'd have to give up for it. And in some ways, I have given up everything, but at the same time, nothing essential is missing. Everything was lost, and even more has been recovered, like things that are carried out to sea and then wash up on the same beach, alongside entirely new and glimmering treasures.

Every life tells a story, through words and actions and choices, through our homes and our children, through our clothes and dishes and perfume. We each play a character in a grand drama, and every stage direction matters. We tell our stories, and we let God's story be told through our stories. We hide and we seek, and we lose ourselves in the best possible way, and find things around us and inside ourselves that we never expected. We tell God's story as we live and discover our own. We know that God is a storyteller. And I don't know if there's anything better in the world than when we lay ourselves wide open and let his story become our story, when we screw up our fists and our courage and start to tell the truest, best stories we know, which are always God's stories.

Where are some of the unlikely places you've experienced God's presence?

DAY 27

The Narrowing

I try to write most mornings—bed-headed and barefoot, pajamas on the porch, coffee next to me, eyes moving from the laptop to the water and back a thousand times. There are plenty of mornings that are just slogging through, like any work. But you sit down and do the work one day—let's say a Thursday—not because you believe anything amazing is going to get written that Thursday, but as a contribution to the muscle memory that will benefit you Friday or Saturday or Sunday or next month.

It's like anything: plain old showing up, reps, running out the clock, because even if all you did was string together a dozen mediocre sentences, maybe tomorrow or the next day your fingers will find that good, generative, muscular rhythm, and it will be because of the slogging through you did today. So slog through, investing your heart and your mind and your fingers in what you might write next week or a month from now. It's worth it.

And don't be afraid to write about a zillion times more words than you need for the project at hand. I write approximately seven whole books for every one that gets published—I believe wholeheartedly in just making sentences, one after another after another and trusting that over time it will become clear which ones to lift out and preserve. A writer friend of mine says he can tell the quality of the work he's doing by what he ultimately leaves out in the editing process. You can always tell, I think, when a speech should have been thirteen good, jam-packed motion-filled minutes but the speaker stretched it to fill the required twenty. Do the opposite, every time: write ten times the words you need and then slice away even the extremely good stuff, so that only the true gold remains.

Like anything worth doing, writing is about so much more than the time you spend in front of your computer. It starts with the way you steward your mind and spirit: sleep, play, reading. It continues with the people you surround yourself with—are they kind? Are they brave? Are they honest? What you read matters and the art you consume matters and the number of other things that you allow to crowd your time matters. Creative work demands more than we imagine—or at least it does for me. There are so many things that I can't do, in order to do good creative work—again, it's that narrowing: don't get up from your chair. Don't sign up for a million good things: stay narrow. Do this particular work in a focused way, and leave everything else undone just for a little while.

How do you support your own creative work? What do you do to steward your mind and spirit?

DAY 28

Prayer and Yoga

Prayer, to me, is sort of like yoga, on several levels. It's good for me and helps me, and to be quite honest, I say I do it way more than I actually do. When someone asks, "Do you do yoga?" I answer, "Absolutely. I love it. It totally makes me feel better."

What I mean, in the strictest sense, is that every week

I intend to go to yoga three times, and I occasionally make it to one class, and I have several pairs of yoga pants, and every once in a while, I do a few sun salutations before bed. So really, I'm yoga-ish.

Prayer, in my life, is similar. If you ask me about prayer, I have the books, the journals, a few transcendent experiences, lots of good reasons why every person should do it, and not a ton of extremely current experiences rushing to mind. I believe in it, conceptually. I feel better when I do it. I believe my life would be better if I did it a lot, like yoga, but when it comes right down to it, I'm prayer-ish.

But something has to get you back to yoga, and something has to get you back to prayer, and in my experience, the surest thing in either case is desperation. I wait until my life has become so completely unlivable and the person I am has become so deeply unmoored from reality and hope and goodness, that I break down and pray.

Unfortunately, though, most of the time what I believe in instead of prayer is my own patched-together sense of how life ought to work. In my system, people who work hard end up okay. Also, people who are smart and careful and keep the batteries in their smoke alarms up to date will be safe. People who order their toast dry and only smoke on very special occasions will be healthy. And so on. This personal worldview has actually functioned reasonably well, though I don't tell anyone about it. I tell them, you know,

God is in control, and we never know where that path leads, and I lean not on my own understanding. But secretly, I do absolutely lean on my own understanding.

The problem is that the worldview I've chosen has melted like butter. I had a plan, and the plan is gone. I did it right, in my own made-up system, and it all came out wrong. So now, out of desperation, I'm back to prayer, sheepishly, because I couldn't make my life work without it. I pray out of sheer lack of options.

I pray because I need to. Because I need to remind myself that there is something up there and that it is good. I pray to be heard, certainly, but practically speaking, what the act of prayer does in my life is profound in its own right. The act and posture of prayer connects me back to something I lose so often, something that gets snipped like a string. Prayer ties up the string one more time. Prayer says, I know you're up there. I believe you. I can make it. I know you are good. To pray is to say that there is more than I can see, and more than I can do.

Prayer, like yoga, like singing, brings soft from hard, pliant from brittle, possible from impossible, warm from cold, breath from breathless. And no matter what gets you there, it is better to be there than not.

How do you think of prayer? How does it make it you feel when you pray?

Shalom

There is a way of living, a way of harmonizing and hitting a balance point, a converging of a thousand balance points and voices, layering together, twisting together, and there are moments when it all clicks into place just for a split second—God and forgiveness and something deep inside that feels like peace—and that's the place I'm trying to get to.

I have glimpses every once in a while of this achingly beautiful way of living that comes when the plates stop spinning and the masks fall off and the apologies come from the deepest places and so do the prayers, and I am fighting to make more of my life that life. I want that happiness that is so much deeper than happy—peace that comes from your toes, that makes you want to live forever, that makes you gulp back sobs because you remember so many moments of so much un-peace. I search for those moments the way I search for beach glass, bits of glitter along a desolate expanse of sand, and I want those moments to stretch into hours, into days.

The word I use for it is *shalom*. It is the physical, sense-oriented, relational, communal, personal, ideological posture that arches God-ward. To get there, I'm finding, is the hardest work and the most worthwhile fight. Shalom requires so much and is something you can't fake, so you have to lay yourself open to it, wide open and vulnerable to what it might ask of you, what it might require you to give up, get over, get outside of, get free from. It feels, sometimes, like running farther than you thought you could run, legs shaking and lungs burning, feeling proud and surprised at what little old you can do.

I have been surprised to find that I am given more life, more hope, more moments of buoyancy and redemption, the more I give up. The more I let go, do without, reduce, the more I feel rich. The more I let people be who they are, instead of cramming them into what I need from them, the more surprised I am by their beauty and depth.

When we can manage to live this way of shalom, even for a moment, we pull each other up toward something bigger, wider, more beautiful, because left to my own devices, chances are, I will spiral down until life is the guilt I feel about all the things I thought I'd be.

The truest thing, it seems, is the biggest: the big idea of making a life with God, with honor, with honesty and community and beauty and the fragile delicate recipe of those, searching for the place where they all come together, where hope and struggle and beauty and tears swirl together into the best, brightest moments of life. That's what I believe about God.

Shalom is happening all around us, but in the same way that forgiveness never feels natural until after it's done, and hope always feels impossible before we commit to it, in the same way that taking is easier than giving, and giving in is easier than getting up, in that same way, shalom never happens on its own.

It happens when we do the hardest work, the most secret struggle, the most demanding truth telling. In those moments of ferocity and fight, peace is born. Shalom arrives, and everything is new. And when you've tasted it, smelled it, fought for it, you'll give your soul to get a little more, and it is always worth it.

What does shalom look like to you?

Not Okay

There is something about summer in Michigan that feels heady and reckless and celebratory, and then something about the pain and fear of hospitals and emergency phone calls that lets a whole lot of things fall away, leaving you with the things that matter when nothing else does.

I unpacked my bags today. There were four of them, from four different trips in the last three weeks. I felt like an archaeologist, unearthing layer after layer of the chronology of the month. I did an insane amount of laundry, as though a football team lived here, instead of just Aaron and me, and I went grocery shopping for the first time in weeks.

The idea that everything is okay is nothing but cruel in its untruth. We live in reasonable peace, accomplishing things and taking that work trip and doing what we're told and expecting that if we behave, we will be rewarded; that for living quietly and industriously, for donating to a non-profit, we will be given good things, good lives. And then something happens to us; we get that phone call or that feeling or that doctor's report, and everything changes.

The sky might as well be red, the solid ground replaced with seawater, because it is a different world. It's like a chemical change, charges reversing from positive to negative. And in the midst of this change, we preserve the myth even though we no longer believe it. We insist that everything is okay. But we're kidding ourselves. Can you look into the eyes of the people around you and really believe that everything is okay? We want to believe that things roll off our backs, that we are tough and world-wise, and that we're all holding it together pretty well. But you know which door you lock behind you when you're crying so hard you can't see. You know what word or image rips off that scab. Everything is not okay.

In all of my scrambling to do the right thing and be the right person, I miss some of the most important things I think God might be asking me to do. For a lot of different reasons, for the better part of the last several years, I have been way too busy for interruptions. I wanted to be productive and useful and focused, and I turned into someone who was frazzled and scattered, and who could not bear the emotional weight of her own life, let alone someone else's. I don't want to be that person.

This week, listening to God and doing what it seemed like he was asking looked a lot like doing nothing, really. I changed plans and bought gifts and said prayers and made my friend dinner, and the most important thing about this is that there is nothing particularly noble or difficult about anything I did. I did the average things that needed to be done in the lives of the people around me. And I think I'm catching on to something that God wanted from me all along.

The bottom just falls out sometimes, and nobody is exempt. Everything is not okay. And one of the most sacred gifts we can offer before God is the willingness to make a bed on the couch or make a phone call or make a meal for someone we care about. I can be there, and I can feed them, and I can listen to their stories. I can sit in silence, knowing that everything is not okay, but that this tiny moment is.

What can you do to make someone else's not okay-ness a little better?

Blessings and Curses

Anyone can celebrate when things are good. But when you realize that the story of your life could be told a thousand different ways, that you could tell it over and over as a tragedy, but you choose to call it an epic, that's when you start to learn what celebration is. When what you see in front of you is so far outside of what you dreamed, but you have the belief, the boldness, the courage to call it beautiful instead of calling it wrong, that's celebration.

When you can invest yourself deeply and unremittingly in the life that surrounds you instead of declaring yourself out of the game, because what's happened to you is too bad, too deep, too ugly for anyone to expect you to move on from, that's that good, rich place. That's the place where the things that looked like curses start to stand up and shimmer and dance, and you realize with a gasp that the force of your belief and your hope and your desperate love for life as it is actually unfolding, has brought a blessing from a curse, like water from a stone, like life from a tomb, like the actual story of God over and over.

I would never try to tell you that every bad thing is really a good thing, just waiting to be gazed at with pretty new eyes, just waiting to be shined up and—ta da!—discovered as fantastic. But what I know is that more often than not, there is something just past the heartbreak, just past the curse, just past the despair, and that thing is beautiful. You don't want it to be beautiful, at first. You want to stay in the pain and the blackness because it feels familiar, and because you're not done feeling victimized and smashed up. But one day you'll wake up surprised and humbled, staring at something you thought for sure was a curse and has revealed itself to be a blessing—a beautiful, delicate blessing.

There have been a thousand moments when I have felt the weight and the sadness of a season appropriately. But then there have been some moments where I have felt the blessing and beauty of it too. There is a particular beauty in this, not the obvious everything-is-perfect beauty, but a strange, slanted pleasantness that surprises me and catches in my throat like a sob or a song.

Nothing good comes easily. You have to lose things you thought you loved, give up things you thought you needed. You have to get over yourself, beyond your past, out from under the weight of your future. The good stuff never comes when things are easy. It comes when things are all heavily weighted down. It comes just when you think it never will, like a shimmering Las Vegas rising up out of the dry desert, sparkling and humming with energy, a blessing that rose up out of a bone-dry, dusty curse.

When I lived in Santa Barbara, every time I drove to Las Vegas, I always got scared that I was lost, that I would die in the desert, eaten by a coyote. The road was desolate, and the truck stops eerie and silent, and I always began to lose hope—there was no Vegas, no city in this bleak desert. We were sure to die, right on the side of the Pearblossom Freeway. And then, every time, there it was, like a mirage, like a glimmering epic gift. We become who we are in these moments.

What good thing in your life has come out of a difficult season?

Possibility

One snowy Monday, when Henry was almost three months old, after a busy week and weekend, we stayed home and wore our pajamas all day. I did laundry while Henry napped, and while he was awake, we played together. There are moments when I swear he understands every word I say, because he looks up at me with a face that seems to say, "I hear you. I get what you're saying, Mom."

When I change him, I talk with him about the day, about current events, about celebrity breakups. Before I put his sleeper back on, I tickled his legs and belly, and I bent down and kissed the bottoms of his feet, because they're so soft and perfect and chubby, and before I knew it, there were tears running down my face, and I cried so hard, I couldn't keep talking to him.

All alone in our house with my son, in the midst of a frantic holiday season, I knew that that moment right there, in the dim corner of the living room on a dark Monday afternoon, that was the merriest Christmas moment for me. The sweetest moment of gratitude and hope happened right then, in our quiet house with my son, kissing his little baby feet.

And it is, after all, a season for babies. It makes sense to me in a new way that God chose to wrap his divinity in baby bones and baby skin. I always thought maybe it was to demonstrate vulnerability, or to identify fully with each phase of humanity, but now I think it was something else. I think it was because babies make us believe in the possibility and power of the future.

It's genius that the Christ, the Messiah, came as a baby,

not because of his helplessness, but because of the possibility every baby holds. When I look at our baby's sleeping face, all the world seems new and possible. It has turned a color I never imagined, and I never dreamed that this little person could capture me so deeply, could change my entire life so completely. This year I lost some things that were very important to me, but in that moment, as I held his little feet, I knew that I had everything the world could possibly give me. Life sneaks up on us every once in a while and gives us something we didn't even know we wanted, and lights within us a love we didn't even know existed.

What has provided you with gratitude and hope and possibility recently?

DAY 33

Ladybugs

All my life I've been multitasking. I'm good at it. I don't want to be braggy, but I'm kind of a champion multitasker, really. And all of a sudden, when I had a baby, what's valuable is not the multitasking, but the single task—being with him, only him, doing nothing else.

It doesn't matter to Henry one little bit that I can speak French or explicate sentences or cook really good roasted salmon. What matters is that I can be there with him as long as he needs me. What matters to him is that I can play with Froggie, his favorite toy, one more time, one more time, one more time.

Writing is the same way. I was good at working, good at the buzz and busyness of leading people and managing events and ideas. What made me good at it was my ability to hold so many things in my head, like a handful of lady-bugs. And now my work, writing, is about letting all the bugs crawl away and being able to focus on a totally blank page, a totally empty hand. Writing is about choosing the one narrow thing and following it as far as it will take me, instead of chasing all the snaps and crackles in my head.

I thought that each of those single tasks, caring for our baby and writing, would make my world very small. What I have found, though, is that they make my world impossibly big, that they open up something in my head and in my heart.

In my grandparents' house, when I was small, there were crystals hung on fishing line over the kitchen sink. They were like small ornaments, light-catchers, and when the sun came through the glass in the mornings, the whole kitchen was filled with bright wiggling rainbows of light, and we were mesmerized by the beauty and magic of it. It was so strange and surprising to us that Grandma's tidy house, with vacuumed carpet lines and fine lace doilies, could become such a wild, beautiful place with all those jumping bands of color. It was like having a disco ball in the kitchen, and it made us giggle and bounce with the sheer energy of all that beauty.

That's how it is now, like these small simple things, this tiny child and this blank screen, have turned the living room into a wonderland, bouncing and brimming over unexpectedly with beauty and color and bands of light.

What has brought you beauty and light?

What in your life would benefit from single focus?

DAY 34

An Apology

I owe my body an apology. Technically, I owe my body thousands of apologies, but now I owe it another one, and I also owe it my gratitude, long overdue, and for the first time, sincere.

I'm sorry for taking you for granted, for wishing you were different, and for abusing you because you looked different than I wanted you to. I'm sorry. And thank you. Thank you for, despite my persecution, being strong and able in the most important way. Thank you for carrying and bearing and nourishing my son.

If bodies lived on love and harmony with the spirits who reside within them, mine would have conked out a long time ago. I fed it a steady diet of hate, venom, and fat-free pseudo food for decades. Poor body. What this collection of blood and guts has been through makes me weep for it now.

I was always a little nervous about being pregnant. First, there's the general nervousness about being able to get pregnant. We spend all these years taking little pills to not get pregnant, and then many of us find out we didn't need them all along. I felt a serious, deep gratitude when I became pregnant.

Then, this body that I had been mad at for over two decades, this body that had been betraying me over and over, this same body was carrying and creating and nourishing another body. This stubborn collection of bones and flesh became a home, a host for an entirely new person during the most crucial time in his life. I was astonished, and humbled.

As I watched my belly grow, I practiced telling myself the things I told my girlfriends when they were pregnant and self-conscious. I told myself that to nourish a small person is a sacred thing, and that the power it takes to grow a person is so much more important than how you look in the process. I told myself that pregnancy is beautiful because of what it represents, that it is a symbol of new life and possibility. I told myself all of these things, and while I agreed with them cognitively, it is much easier to believe them now that I am no longer pregnant.

What changed my mind and body, in a very serious way, was the actual experience of birth. What bodies can do in those moments will take your breath away. Henry's birth felt sacred and overwhelming and full of beauty and prayer. And the fact that this body was able to do that thing silences all those voices that have been yelling at it for years.

This body might not look like much on the outside, and believe me, post-baby, it doesn't. But it did what it came to do on that day, and for that, I am grateful, and for that, I offer it my most sincere apologies.

What does apologizing to your body look like?

Writing in Pencil

I'm finally willing to admit something about life, or at least about my life, and it's this: I should have written in pencil. I should have viewed the trajectory of my life as a mystery or an unknown. I should have planned lightly, hypothetically, and should have used words like "maybe" and "possibly." Instead, every chance I got, I wrote in stone and Sharpie. I stood on my future, on what I knew, on the certainty of what life would hold for me, as though it was rock. What I know now is that instead of rock, it's more like a magic carpet, a slippy-slidy-wiggly thing, full of equal parts play and terror. The ground beneath my feet is lurching and breaking, making way for an entirely new thing every time I look down. I am surprised once again by a future I couldn't have predicted.

Life with God at its core is about giving your life up to something bigger and more powerful. It's about saying at every turn that God knows better than we know, and that his Spirit will lead us in ways that we couldn't have predicted. I have known that, but I haven't really lived that.

There is a loosey-goosey feeling to the future now, both a slight edge of anxiety, like anything can happen, and a slight bubble of hope and freedom that, well, anything can happen. There are moments when I feel, suddenly, lucky and thankful and shocked at how happy I am. I am in the middle of a season that is not what I had planned in the least, but it is also a secretly beautiful, special season at the same time. I am afraid, sometimes, about the future, but at the same time, I surprise myself with how okay it is and how okay I am with not knowing exactly what will come next.

That's what I want. I want to arrive. I want to get to wherever I'm going and stay there. That's why I was such a ferocious planner of my life. But I'm learning to just keep moving, keep walking, keep taking teeny tiny steps. And it's in those teeny tiny steps and moments that I become, actually, who I am. We won't arrive. But we can become. And that's the most hopeful thing I can think of.

Thank God I was wrong about everything I had planned. Thank God we weren't on my schedule, because even though I dragged my heels and checked my planner every five seconds while I watched my life change in his hands, I really like the place we've ended up, and the things I've seen along the way. Now when I think about the future, I try to write in pencil.

What, in hindsight, did you realize that you should have written in pencil?

The Interim

I went for a walk a few months ago with my friend Rosa. She was an elder at our church and has four kids. Her husband owns a successful dental practice, and they have a beautiful home where they entertain a lot. The last few years they were traveling more and more, helping churches all over the world, and recently decided to move to North Africa with their kids.

As we talked about it, I commented that this season, while they're selling their house and getting ready to move, must feel like an interim season. And she stopped for a second and looked at me pointedly. "You know, Shauna," she said, "everything is interim. Every season that I thought was stable and would be just how it was for a long time ended up being a preparation or a path to the next thing. When you decide to be on this journey with God, everything is interim." When I got back home, I wrote that phrase on a Post-It and keep it near my computer.

Everything is interim. Everything is a path or a preparation for the next thing, and we never know what the next thing is. Life is like that, of course, twisty and surprising. But life with God is like that exponentially. We can dig in, make plans, write in stone, pretend we're not listening, but the voice of God has a way of being heard. It seeps in like smoke or vapor even when we've barred the door against any last-minute changes, and it moves us to different countries and different emotional territories and different ways of living. Life with God is a daring dream, full of flashes and last-minute exits and generally all the things we've said we'll never do. And with the surprises comes great hope.

When it comes right down to it, of course, it's always been in the interim. We've always been in the middle space, the not-yet-heaven middle space, the yearning and groaning. We construct elaborate castles of business cards and Pottery Barn catalogs, and craft armor out of skinny jeans and insurance policies and text messages, beating back the sense that we are not enough, that life is not offering us enough, but we are not and it isn't.

All of life is in the interim, and if we're honest and tender with ourselves, if the armor is off and the castle has crumpled, we feel the ache of the meantime. Our permanent records are a mess of marks and offenses, and we are laid bare to the ache of what's coming.

What can you do to live more wholeheartedly in the interim?

Consider the Leaves

Just this morning, a friend discovered that I am not a fall person—and what followed was horror and disbelief. *What about sweaters? Crisp mornings? Bonfires? Football?*

Without fail, whenever someone discovers this opinion of mine, they start listing things about fall that *they* love, as though I wasn't aware of them and now I might be convinced. *Oh, wait—soup? I had no idea! Consider me a convert!*

While fall will never be my favorite season, I did start looking at all the seasons and asking what I can learn from each one. I started to see fall as a time of invitation—every season, of course, contains all sorts of invitations, but if I'm honest, autumn's invitations are the easiest for me to ignore.

You know how I feel about summer's invitations: *Play! Jump in! Soak up the sunshine!* Not a problem for this solar-powered girl.

I'm down with spring's invitations: *Bloom! Begin! Keep your eyes peeled and your heart open for signs of new life, even tiny ones.* I got it—I can get into spring.

I'm even pretty good at winter's invitations: *Hush. Get cozy. Stay in.* This bookworm loves a candle and a blanket and a good book on a cold night.

Autumn, though, is the toughest for me, because the invitation of autumn is to let go, and letting go is not my strong suit. I'm a go-down-with-the-ship stage-five-clinger. I tend to overstay in relationships, in jobs, in houses, and towns. I've let fear and nostalgia and familiarity keep me clinging to what I know instead of walking into the unknown.

But here we are, the season of letting go, and I really do believe that part of being a grower is learning from every season, not just the ones that appeal to us or come easily.

And so this morning I'm considering the leaves: they grow in spring, they dance in summer, and then in the fall, they blaze into color and *let go*.

Winter is about quiet, about stillness, about simplicity. In order to get from the full-tilt, wide-open embrace of summer to the quiet simplicity of winter, you have to follow the pattern of autumn—you have to let some things go.

Here's to letting go, in order to make space for what's next.

What is it in my life that I need to let go?

Thanksgiving

One snowy night halfway through December, we hosted housechurch at our house, and in a fit of good intentions, I decided to cook a Thanksgiving dinner. I realized that I wanted to celebrate the holiday with them. We talk about being one another's family, and that has become so true that when a family time comes, like a holiday, it doesn't feel right to spend it without them.

I wanted to do the thanks part, the part where you stop and think about the year, and think about what you're thankful for, or what you've been given, or the gratitude you feel toward the people you love and to God for his good gifts.

I set the table all fancy, with silver chargers and balloon wine glasses and silver candlesticks with long red tapers, and a platter on the coffee table with seven flutes of champagne. When the turkey finally decided to be done, after a zillion years, we sat in the twinkly, candlelit dining room and ate and talked about the time we'd spent with our families over the holiday, about the things that change and the things that never do.

What I've found this year, though, is a different kind

of gratitude. I am thankful, I realized in those moments, thankful for the breaking of things that needed to be broken, that couldn't have been broken any other way, thankful for the severing that allowed me to fall all the way down to the center of my fear and look it in the face, thankful for being set free from something I didn't even know I was enslaved to. There is a quality in my life that I sense now, like a rumbling bass line, or thunder faraway, and the only phrase I can find to capture it is that it is the feeling of having nothing to lose. And to my surprise, I'm still here. I'm happy in a new way, free in a new way.

I am all the clichés that made me so mad several months ago. I believe in the gift of pain. I believe that loss deepens us. I am grateful for God's graciousness toward me that he would teach me these things. And I could gag at that sentence, for how Pollyanna it sounds. As much as I hate to admit it, I've found a new gratitude, and it's gratitude for the way God has redeemed darkness and pain, for the way he brings something beautiful out of something horrible. That's the kind of gratitude we talked about on our snowy Thanksgiving night.

We talked about the ways that God's hand has reached through the darkness in each of our lives. And in those moments, we became more than the sum of our parts, and more than we had been, previously, as a community.

While our babies slept upstairs, and the leftovers and

turkey bones littered the table, we told the stories that no one tells, the stories of the darkest places, the most painful moments, and the ways God has held those moments up and turned them from ash to luminous things, treasures, shards of hope.

When we stood in a circle to pray and close our night together, we held hands and thanked God for the darkness, and for the way the darkness had become light, and in that moment, we practiced Thanksgiving. Thanksgiving for the uncomplicated happiness of babies and friendship and food, and for the very complicated joys that come from loss, from failure, from reaching the bottom and pushing back up to the light.

What unexpected things are you thankful for?

Soup from Bones

Some little girls loved Barbies or Cabbage Patch Kids. I loved the *Little House on the Prairie* books. Not the show so much, but the books. I got them for my sixth birthday in a yellow cardboard box set and reread them every year.

Making soup from bones seemed to me like something that Ma would do in the winter, while Pa was shoveling the roof, or breaking the icicles from the cows' noses so they didn't freeze.

I consulted my *How to Cook Everything* and took some suggestions, which is as close as I get to following a recipe. I chopped garlic, onions, carrots, and celery and boiled the bones in my big red soup pot. I added some leftover turkey and a handful of rice, and all of a sudden, soup!

And that soup, that plain old turkey soup, made me feel like a miracle worker or a magician, bringing something from nothing. It's a very practical act of redemption. It's essentially making a meal out of things that would otherwise become garbage. I think there's a particular beauty to that idea for me right now because I've spent so long feeling like a pile of bones, and the idea that these old bones can make something lovely and sustaining moves me.

That's the heart of the story, really, the story of God and people and his hands in the world. All through history, he's making soup from bones, life from death, water from rocks, love from hate.

I like the idea of everything being alive, healthy, brimming with spirit and hope. I wish my life was like that. There are moments of life and beauty, but there are also a lot of bones, skeletons from lives already lived, regrets, broken hearts and promises and relationships. Now on my best days, I take a look at each pile of bones and imagine what it would take to make some soup, to repair and redeem, to make something dead into something full of life and flavor.

Sometimes it takes a phone call, or an apology. Sometimes it takes a new promise, even though I've broken so many in the past. Sometimes telling the truth, sometimes giving up something important, sometimes leaving something long dead. And what you get from that pile of bones is soup—warm, rich, full of life and soul and spirit. You get something beautiful out of bones, which is the whole point.

When was the last time you made something beautiful out of bones?

Prayer as a Refuge

The holidays strike me as especially beautiful this year, the twinkly trees and wreaths, the bright winks of candles in menorahs. I'm finding myself more drawn than ever to the traditions and songs and, really, the tenderness of the season.

Maybe it's because there is so much loss. Maybe it's

because it feels like there's darkness nearly everywhere we look, and it makes the gentle candle flames and beautiful sounds and smells and rhythms all the more sacred and beautiful. Maybe we need the story of the baby and the manger more desperately than ever. Maybe it's always this way—I don't know, but I feel both the beauty and the weight of this season more deeply than ever.

I'm finding myself so moved by the little things—the lights on our tree, especially in the evenings. The cookies in my cute cookie tin, symbols of love and care from my neighbors and from my mom, who sent me home with gingerbread because she knows how much Henry and I love it. The cards that arrive every day from friends around the country—kids taller every year, sweet messages scribbled on the back. I love getting the mail and opening the cards and gathering them in a little basket on our table by the tree. They mean more to me this year—it feels like everything does.

In the same way, I'm finding myself looking to prayer as a refuge. I think this mostly in the night, to be honest, so when I'm awake in the night, I pray. Sometimes I repeat one phrase from scripture over and over, matching my breath to the phrase. Sometimes I listen for the loving stillness of God's presence, and sometimes I ramble on and on about all the things that feel out of control in my life and in the world. Sometimes I imagine placing the things that feel heavy in my life into a loving hand—into God's loving hand.

Prayer, in this beautiful and difficult season, is one of the greatest gifts and refuges in my life, and I absolutely cannot recommend it enough. Prayer is nothing more and nothing less than a loving conversation with the divine. It's an opening of the heart and spirit, an invitation, a sacred listening. It's drawing close to the sacred presence of Christ who cares for you and tends to you, a presence in which you can rest and be young and tired and small, instead of having to be big and expert and full of answers. Prayer feels, to me, like climbing into a safe, soft place, like being held and comforted like a child. I love it, and I need it, and it's one of the most nourishing practices of my life.

The good news is that the heart of God is bent close and listening to us fragile and tired humans. The divine presence accompanying us on the journey. The sacred invitation to exhale, held by a power greater than our own.

And so I'm not saying you *should* pray, like you should take your vitamins or you should eat your vegetables. I'm saying you *can* pray—what a gift. What a delight. What a refuge.

When do you find that you turn to prayer?

How has prayer changed you?

Let It Be

During Christmas, we often focus on the difficulty of what Mary was asked to do—the weight of it, the loneliness, the giving up of what she thought her life and future would be in exchange for a plan from an angel. We focus on the hard thing, but I will confess that sometimes I want what Mary had: I want an angel, and I want an assignment. I want can't-miss-it clarity, a special purpose, the certainty that I'm on the right path, doing the right thing, and that it matters.

I will confess that sometimes I want an angel to show up and tell me exactly what to do. How great would it be if you could carry with you the memory of a visit from an angel, if every time your calling felt too hard or too heavy, you could go back to God's actual words to you, you could hold them like a coin every time you felt scared or small or weary?

We want angels and assignments, and instead we just have our own lives and neighborhoods and jobs and families. But wait.

The theologian Eugene Peterson said that to eyes that see, every bush is a burning bush. And maybe in that same way, there are angels and assignments all around us, and the trick is to be the kind of people who see them.

Is it possible that your divine assignment is your actual life, right now? Is your angel a child who needs extra care, a neighbor in need of support, a song that begs to be composed, a painting that is still a blank canvas?

Could it be that we have all been visited and assigned, but we dismissed all that as plain old life, preferring to wait for something spectacular and clear?

Your calling today, right now, is as clear and urgent as Mary's: today, right now, use what you have and who you are and what you love and what you've learned—use your bruises and your scars and your dreams to serve and heal the world today. And then do it again tomorrow.

Open your eyes to what's broken and missing and wrecked all around you and use everything you have to heal it up, repair it, rebuild it.

Maybe there are angels and assignments everywhere, if you learn to see with new eyes. We don't get the certainty and drama of Mary's visitation, but that doesn't mean there aren't invitations all around us, every day, every hour.

This is what I think: I think there are little angels and small assignments masquerading as just plain life—my life, your life. There are hands that need holding, lonely people who need comforting, wounds that need tending, mouths that need feeding, hearts that need healing, songs that need writing, sidewalks that need shoveling. These are the angels and the assignments all around us.

And my prayer today is that we will respond to those little angels and small assignments with the faith and bravery that Mary did all those years ago: Let it Be.

We want drama and certainty. What we get is much quieter than that, much more confusing sometimes, much messier. And to that I say: Let it Be.

Let's hold out our hands and accept the mystery and challenges and callings of our own lives, and our own angels, and our own assignments: let it be.

> What are a few of the small assignments that have been given to you?

DAY 42

It's Okay to Cry

This is a season of so much transition for so many people in my life, and wise people have reminded me that the only way through the most difficult passages is right through the middle—not skirting the edges, not tiptoeing out of bounds, not staying stuck in the same place hoping for a different outcome.

And part of braving these passages is letting yourself

feel it, whatever it is: the anger, the joy, the sadness, the hope. I have a tendency to feel big feelings but really quick, like a squall that screams across the lake full of wind and lightning, gone as quickly as it came. And in recent years good friends have whispered to me, as only really good friends can do, "Nice try, pumpkin. You're not even close to through with this one, so settle in for a while."

And then there are other days when you've been in the dark and the loss for what seems like forever, and all of a sudden you realize you just laughed or felt joy or a spring of hope, and you look around to see if the sad police are going to come issue you a ticket for daring to be joyful when someone told you that you were only allowed to be sad, sad, sad.

But not only is it okay to feel joy right in the middle of the darkest seasons, it's necessary. Joy is a part of reality every much as pain is—beautiful, healthy babies are being born, dreams are coming to life, people are falling in love, hearts are being stitched back together, and all of those things are worth marking and celebrating, especially in the hardest stretches.

And so, whatever these days hold for you: feel it, all of it. Let it work through your life like yeast through dough, transforming you, delivering you to a new reality, even if it's not one you chose. This is how it is, for all of us: loving something, letting go, beginning again. Again. Again. Again.

Grieve what's gone. Inch toward what's new. Cry. Let go. Hope.

Sometimes all in the same day.

Sometimes all in the same breath.

Looking back on a hard time, what and/or who were the bright spots of joy? How did they help you through?

Hard Days

When I'm having a hard day, I fall back on a few life-giving routines that are important in order to feel better and to get back on track.

The first routine is to shower. Okay, if you're a person who showers every single morning, you can skip this paragraph, but anyone who knows me well knows that I sometimes go a really terrifying amount of time without a shower, especially in the winter. Here's my theory: I want to be warm and dry. And if I skip a shower, I stay warm and dry. If I shower, I get wet and cold, and that's the opposite of warm and dry. But when I'm out of sorts, a shower is a great reset, no matter the time of day. It's like starting over. Water just holds mood-changing magic. I also highly recommend a glass of water and going out of your way to even get a glimpse of the water. When we're in South Haven, lots of times I drive through the beach parking lot and sit for a few minutes and watch the water.

Another thing that helps on hard days is to make a big salad. My preference is a huge, chopped salad with like fifteen ingredients, but find what works for you. Some of why it helps, I think, is because the chopping always makes me feel a little better, like I'm taking care of myself the way I'd take care of someone else. Today after I dropped Henry off at school, I stopped at the grocery store for baby spinach and a few other things, and when I got home, I opened the kitchen window, and set out the cutting board in the morning light. A little bit of onion, diced fine. A half a can of chickpeas, an apple, some English white cheddar. Lots of spinach, some roasted and salted almonds, roughly chopped, and a vinaigrette shaken together in a jam jar. I ate one bowl for breakfast, and will eat another for lunch, a way of telling myself that I'm worth feeding, worth taking care of.

Finally, be on the hunt for beauty: take an extra minute to light the good candles or make your bed or put something way. When things are dark for me, I tend to disconnect from everything: let the dishes stack up, ignore the stack of mail, slam the pantry door against the mounting recycling pile. But it makes me feel better to just do these things, to create a little order in my space. I'm very affected by my environment, which is not always a good thing. I have a couple friends who live like turtles, almost, everything they need and feel inside themselves, compact and self-sufficient. I feel more like a strip of scotch tape, picking up and gathering everything with my, absorbing feelings and sounds and smells, collecting it all and letting all those things out there tell me how it feels in here. Now that I know that about myself, I can start to feel better when I actively engage in my environment instead of feeling steamrolled by it. If I engage in making a beautiful, joyful space, I can recover or locate some of my own sense of beauty and joy.

> What do you do to change your mood when you're having a bad day?

DAY 44

Waking Up

There were whole years, during which I woke up and just seconds after waking, I knew, in a deep sense, everything I needed to know: this is who I am. This is where I am. This is what I want. This is the world as I know it, the solid ground beneath my feet, the stories and beliefs and ideas that I wrap around myself like a blanket.

Sometimes I wake up, and there are a few long seconds of blankness that turn to terror. And it's like I wake up disassembled, and the process of waking up is reattaching my arms and my legs, finding my fingers or feet, building a whole self again, every morning—no givens, no understandings, no carryover from yesterday.

What I need is a new dream, a new vision. I find myself longing for control, certainty, plans. I want to nail things down, have answers, fill in the blanks of the calendar.

I asked myself the question, as a part of my spiritual practice: is there anything in my life that requires me to pretend? Anything unfaced? Any truth I don't want to admit to myself? What is it that's clear about my life but that I haven't yet been able to face or fear or say? What is it that everyone else can see but me?

So many of my moments of greatest happiness were just those—moments: a boat ride or a book or an evening, a meal, a dinner. In the midst of a difficult day or month or season, sometimes all you can do is hold on to a moment of brightness or beauty in the midst of the darkness.

Today though, I woke up and there's something light in my spirit, something that sees the possibility for joy, for happiness, for truly leaving things behind. I'd started to fear that this moment would never come, and here it is:

something like pushing up from the bottom. I feel almost an otherworldly, magical sense of hope and optimism, like it's possible our future will be good, and we'll love our life, even though it's not the one we imagined. We'll make something new from the dust of what's been broken, and it won't be the same, but it will be lovely and meaningful in its own way—that's the miracle.

Your life as you knew it can unravel entirely, and you can make it through. You can keep showing up, tender and tired and brave. I know that people can break your heart, and the stories that have held the scaffolding for your whole worldview can collapse, and you can make it through. You can keep bowing your head in prayer, keep believing in goodness, keep going.

How do you keep showing up in big and small ways during a difficult season?

On Resilience

My love for resilience comes out of the fact that it's the skill I've needed and used a thousand times. Creativity, flexibility, adaptability—those are all functions of resilience, and I can't think of almost anything that can serve us better. This is resilience: falling and getting up. And falling and getting up. And falling and getting up.

The good news is that the ability to rise after a fall is a skill that can be taught. We can teach ourselves how to rise after a failure. It's something we can all learn and practice, and it's disproportionately important. We see this, especially in professional sports. A scout, if deciding between two players—if one has superior skills, but the other has a better developed ability to reset, the scout will choose the player who can reset. It's that valuable.

Aaron is a 4th generation Chicago Cubs fan, and we definitely bleed Cubby Blue. One of our favorite players is Javier Baez; they call him El Mago, the magician. I heard an interview with Joe Maddon, who was the Cubs manager for a long time, and he said what's so special about Javi is that he has no short-term memory. He swings at a bad pitch and immediately forgets about it before the next pitch crosses the plate. Madden says that Javi doesn't take a bad moment into the next moment. That's resilience. That's bounce.

There is so much falling right now, and so much more rising. But here's the good news: it gets easier the more we do it. Our brain rewires itself to problem solve, and it doesn't just change us; it changes us so that we can be a part of changing the world around us.

Several years ago, my friend was hiking in a forest preserve near her house, and out of nowhere, a large branch broke above her, and it fell on her and knocked her to the ground, unconscious. She shouldn't have lived through it. It took many months for her to recover physically.

And she realized that a physical recovery was not the only thing she needed. As she laid in her hospital bed, she said, *If I live through this, I'm not going back to my old life.* She began to make very difficult changes, ones that she'd been afraid to make for a long time. She went back to school. She rebuilt her life on her own terms, from a place of authenticity and wholeness. And then she became a therapist to walk alongside people as they make their own difficult and necessary choices.

All those years ago, she learned how to get back up, and because she did that work, now she's able to offer her wisdom and guidance to so many people who feel trapped on the ground, unable to rise. While I don't believe that everything happens for a reason, I do believe that everything comes with an invitation. When we learn to rise, we get to show other people how to rise, too.

When have you had to learn resilience? How can you use your experience to help others?

The Practice of Presence

The practice of presence is about embracing reality, about living honestly right here and right now. A wise friend of mine says that true spiritual maturity is nothing more and nothing less than consenting to reality—I love that. I love it, and to be honest, for most of my life, I've been terrible at it.

Recently I hurt my leg. I wish I could tell you that I hurt it training for a marathon or practicing aerial yoga or something exciting, but the truth is, I bent down and felt a sharp pain in my calf muscle. Braided in with the physical pain was frustration and shame . . . how old *am* I? How out of shape *am* I?

My first impulse was to ignore it, walk it out, keep going—business as usual. I mentioned it to my husband, and he teased me lovingly, joking about my tendency to push through and end up prolonging the pain I was trying so hard to ignore.

Crazy idea, he said, *What if this time you did something wild, like stay off of it? Hear me out: What if you rested, and let yourself heal, and also didn't beat yourself up and make yourself feel bad for being hurt?*

Nope, I said, *I think I'm going to stay with my normal two-pronged plan of shaming myself and pretending nothing's wrong.* I smiled. This is a conversation we've been having for years—it's hard for me to admit pain, fragility, weakness of both the physical and spiritual varieties. So I ignore reality and usually end up making it worse.

In a surprising turn of events, though, I followed Aaron's advice. Instead of walking to the grocery store with a friend, I asked her if we could meet for coffee. I changed dinner plans so that I'd only have to walk a few blocks, instead of a few miles.

And then I woke up the next morning and felt notably, considerably better. This was a whole new world to me: honoring my body, feeling my feelings, consenting to reality. It's a silly example, of course, but I've spent most of my life pushing through pain, both physical and otherwise, and choosing to honor my body and my feelings is still something like a new trick—I'm always a little shocked when it works.

For all of us who've been taught to push through, pretend, and perform, *the practice of presence* has the potential to be a life-changing one. If you've been rewarded, like many of us have, for denying your feelings and pushing down pain, this practice is a revelation, an invitation to an entirely new way of living.

In what ways can you honor your body and try the practice of presence?

True Hospitality

Hospitality has been my great love as long as I can remember. A house full of people makes me disproportionately happy, and no matter the circumstances or challenges, I'll find a way to celebrate life's most important moments with the people I love as often as possible.

Hospitality is powerful. It can move us. It can heal us. It can remind us that we're loved, that we matter, that someone cares we're alive.

Hospitality is not entertaining, not performing. It's not about perfection or competition or knocking yourself out to impress someone.

Hospitality is holding space for another person to be seen and heard and loved. It's giving someone a place to be when they'd otherwise be alone. And according to my friend Sibyl, true hospitality is when someone leaves your home feeling better about themselves, not better about you. I feel that in my bones because something miraculous happens when we gather. There's a connection, a healing, a nourishing that goes beyond the nutrients and calories and vitamins and minerals. There's a nourishing of spirit. We need to laugh together and cry together and sit in silence together. We were made for connection, for sitting shoulder to shoulder, for carrying one another, walking together.

We've all experienced that phenomenon of getting used to people who are different than we are—at first, all you see are the differences and you sometimes trip over yourself trying to make sense of languages or accents or traditions that feel unfamiliar, but then over time, what was once foreign starts to feel very normal, like just another part of your world.

Hospitality, which requires bravery, intention, and a willingness to extend beyond ourselves in service of others.

This is hospitality—it's creating a sense of connection and familiarity. It's making something more beautiful and more whimsical and more special than, strictly speaking, it needs to be.

It's about those choosing to invest meaning and beauty in those little moments. It's about seeing someone, inviting them into a place of belonging, making space for their most tender and fearful selves to rest a little bit. That's the true center, the beating heart of hospitality.

But are we showing hospitality to ourselves? A friend of mine put it to me this way: *Shauna, you love to show hospitality to all kinds of people—loud people, messy people, toddlers. Picky eaters, people who don't know when to leave—all kinds of really kooky guests. But over the years, I've watched you really hold some parts of your own self at arms-length. What will it take to show hospitality to even the parts of yourself you don't want to invite in?*

She was so right. I kept pretending everything was all okay, telling a great story to gloss over the cracks. I needed to show hospitality to the parts of myself and my life and my story that I most desperately wanted to ignore.

There's just one self—the self that works and parents and cares for aging parents. It's the same self who goes running or loves to cook or worries about your kids or loves gardening. We need to tend to our whole selves. We need to tend to our health—physical and mental—and our relationships. We need to show hospitality to ourselves so we can, in turn, show true hospitality to others.

What parts of your life do you need to show a little hospitality to? What needs tending? What needs support?

Following the Shepherd

I believe there are moments for prose and moments for poetry, and this season is one for poetry—poetry is the language of unknowing, of scratching at the edges of a feeling or an idea, instead of plunging in with organized, neat sentences.

I love Mary Oliver's beautiful poem, *When Death Comes.* That last line: "I don't want to end up simply having visited this world."

I don't want to hide out, protected by wealth and health, dipping my toes into the very shallow end of life. I don't want to spend my life pretending and posing, hiding myself and my weakness. I don't want to avoid or shy away from all the things in this world that make me scared and uncomfortable.

I don't want to be so concerned with being perceived as smart or independent or shiny or strong that I miss the call of the shepherd, and his vision, not just for me but for all of us, for the thriving and dignity and healing of all of us.

I want to be humble and tender and brave enough to follow the shepherd, to see, in the poet's words, each body a lion of courage, and something precious to this earth. I want to follow the shepherd and take the world into my arms.

Jesus shows us how we were made to interact with one another. Where we all understand ourselves as more similar than different, as interdependent and interconnected. Where status and power are not conferred upon only some, but where the healthy and the sick, the imprisoned and the free, the established and the immigrant live together with love and dignity. This is the way of Jesus. This is God's heart for every nation, in every century, in every part of the world.

We live in a culture that elevates one and renders the other invisible. We give status to one and stigma to the other. And the work for every Christian is to follow the lead of our shepherd, away from status and stigma, away from us and them, away from powerful and powerless. We follow our shepherd as we express the dignity, the beauty, and the immeasurable worth of every human life.

What are you doing to bring Jesus' vision—where everyone is seen and cared for and valued—to reality?

Fragility

I work with a team of people, offering training and skill development to leaders and teams. We invite people into conversations about courage and leadership and integrity, and one of the requirements of this team is that you don't just teach other people these skills and practices—you have practice them. You have to know this work deep in your bones.

And so from time to time, we gather together and some of it feels like training and some of it feels a lot like group therapy. Some of the work our team did together was on the topic of unwanted identities.

Essentially, each of us, for all different reasons, has a couple identities that we would like to avoid. *You can call me this or that, but if you think I'm this one thing, it strikes to the very core of who I so desperately don't want to be.*

We are a team of both men and women, from all over the world. We range in age from our twenties to our seventies. We have different professional backgrounds, religious backgrounds, cultural and political perspectives. And yet, the common denominator for nearly all of our unwanted identities came down to one thing: weakness. Fragility. The need to be protected.

All of us, no matter our background, had a profound aversion to being perceived as weak, fragile, or in need of help.

I think something cyclical happens: when you only see, when you live in a culture that only values the wealthy, the healthy, the free and the established, you begin to hate the parts of yourself that are different than that. You hide those parts, and you don't want to be reminded of them.

But what if we lived in a world where both sides healthy/wealthy/free and also poor/sick/imprisoned were seen, and cared for, and valued?

Many of us find ourselves wanting to hide those weaker or more fragile sides of ourselves, to align as much as possible with this dominant, powerful group. We want to show our shiny selves, not our weak or sick selves. Because sick equals invisible. Poor equals invisible. Imprisoned equals invisible.

But Jesus says, that's not the world that I'm inviting you into. That's not my imagination for what a whole and thriving culture looks like.

Jesus wants us to see and embrace and include every aspect of our humanity—the healthy and the sick, the rich and the poor, the founders and stake-holders and also the immigrants and the refugees, those who have power, and those who have none.

Because Jesus' way of living is able to hold it all. No hiding or pretending. No distancing or othering. If we all were able to see the world as Jesus does, there wouldn't be stigma or shame attached to some categories, and there wouldn't be status and value connected to others. All human. All valued. All seen. All welcome.

> What do you most desperately not want to have someone say about you? What does that reveal about you?

Basement

I haven't told my friend Annette that I saw her basement. I don't think she wants to know. I didn't mean to see her basement, but I was bringing Henry over, and on my way in, I knocked over a stepladder with the car seat, and the stepladder knocked over the broom, which clattered all the way down the basement stairs. Such is life with a car seat.

This is the thing about Annette's basement: it looks surprisingly like my own. And that makes me feel so much better about myself that I want to lay down on the floor for a while and just breathe in the okayness that floods through me.

I don't know if there are things in your life that are harbors and safe houses for all your shame and secrets, things that you would just die if anyone saw or knew about, but for me, my basement is like the holding area for everything that's wrong with my life, all the broken-down bits and pieces that I have banished from my upstanding, upstairs life, but still lurk, threatening to expose me, in the basement.

My basement is all the things that I don't want you to know, that I want to keep covered and out of your sight. I want you to see my living room and my dining room, my best selves, my most charming and evolved selves. But down there, down in the musty, smelly basement are the parts of me that make me embarrassed and sad. Down there are my easily hurt feelings, my adolescent heartbreaks, my public failures, the times I've tried to tell a joke and no one laughed. Down there are the unrequited loves, the left-out feelings, the times when I heard other girls talking about me in the bathroom, both in high school and at church not that long ago. The basement is where all the hidden parts are.

And I want to keep it hidden and have kept it hidden quite successfully. Until this year. Until people I love wanted to help me, and I realized in a panic-stricken moment that if I allowed them to help me, they would see my basement. They would see my basement, and then they would leave, scared and disapproving, shaking their heads and clucking their tongues, knowing that there was always something off about me, come to think of it. They would talk about me in hushed tones, saying, "We should have known about someone like her. We should have guessed she'd have one of *those* basements."

That's why Annette's basement healed me so deeply. Because she's one of the other kind of people. She wears pretty makeup and necklaces and cute shoes. She reapplies lipstick throughout the day and has dress coats and china. She's strong and direct and knows how to do spreadsheets and started her own business.

Her basement doesn't bother me one bit. It's messy and dirty, and you have to wind your way through it like a corn maze, and it doesn't even put a dent in how much I love her and respect her and think she's smart. That makes me feel both honest, like she's seen the very worst and there's nothing else to be exposed; and safe, like she's not going to leave or make fun of me. When you find those things coexisting peacefully in one friendship, I think you've got a good thing going there, and you should let them see your basement.

What are some of your flaws that your friends accept wholeheartedly? What are some of your friends' flaws that make you feel like they're human too?

A Healing Vision

In the parable of the sheep and the goats, Jesus offers us a beautiful and healing vision for what a nation could be. This is a loving leader inviting his followers to share his sacred and radical imagination for a better way to be a community, a more whole and healed way of being than the empire that ruled their lives.

Jesus says that a nation that cares only for the healthy, wealthy, free, and established, is out of balance. And that's a refrain we see throughout Jesus' teachings—it's not enough to just do what most people and most nations do. He's inviting us to imagine a much wider, much more beautiful, totally different way of building a culture, of using power.

We can find comfort in this while living in a culture that largely renders sick people invisible. If you've been sick for a long time, there may have been moments when you wonder, does anyone care about the pain I'm feeling? Has everyone forgotten the weight of illness and what it's done to my life and in this parable, Jesus says: I see you. And I care about you. And any nation shaped according to my vision will care about you too.

For any of us who love someone who has gone to prison or is currently in prison, it's easy to wonder, has that person I love been forgotten? Do they matter to anyone but me? Jesus says, I see you, even in prison. And my vision for a healthy nation includes caring for your needs, too.

For any of us who have, or love someone who has, emigrated—left the countries and traditions and homes you were raised in, and have come here, and Jesus' vision is that you would not be treated as an exile, but like a neighbor. Not an intruder, but a brother or sister.

And many of us have either experienced poverty first-hand, or care deeply for people who have or are living in poverty now. In our culture, the pain of poverty is deepened by the added pain of invisibility, and again, what this parable reminds all of us is that the way of Jesus forces us to see not just the wealthy, but the poor, not just the firmly established, but the immigrant, not just the free, but the prisoner, and not just the healthy, but the sick.

Why do we avoid and distance ourselves from those groups? Why do we downplay those aspects of our own experience, or those identities in ourselves?

It's easy to see only the shiny, polished, pretty have-it-all-together people. It's more difficult to face the open wounds of poverty and illness, because we don't want to be reminded of our own vulnerability, our own shame or weakness or failings.

What are specific ways that you could move toward these groups Jesus mentions—in proximity, in relationship, in service?

And what are some ways that you can consciously unhook yourself from the power of these dominant identities?

Sheep and Goats

I recently spoke with my friend who is raising a pack of twelve fainting goats in Holland, Michigan. Sheep are known for being docile, easy to herd, but to be honest, a little bit dumb. Goats, on the other hand, are incredibly intelligent, resistant to authority outside their pack, and have a reputation for destroying things.

When I spoke to her, it was like talking to any mom who really loves her kids but also definitely knows what's up. I told her how I've read that goats have a reputation for being violent and mean and destructive. And she said, *Oh, I wouldn't say destructive—I would say curious.* And then she added, *But, yeah, they definitely will step on and head butt each other's babies.*

Sheep and goats have to be separated for at least two reasons: first, because goats will injure sheep. The way goats interact with each other is quite violent, and it's okay among the goats but sheep just weren't made that way, and they get badly injured if they're left in the same pen as goats.

Also, the way that a shepherd interacts with each kind of animal is completely different. A shepherd's job is to protect the sheep from their environment. And a shepherd's job is to protect the environment from the goats. Also: when building a fence for goats, the rule is, if water can get through, so can a goat.

We live in a culture that values these goat characteristics— intelligence, independence, toughness, willingness to break any obstacle in our path. This is like action hero stuff. American Dream stuff—I'll do it my way, I'll look out for myself, I don't need help, and I don't need to be told what to do.

But sheep, in our culture, do not enjoy the same respect. We refer to people as sheeple—when we feel like they blindly follow their leader. We denigrate people who need to be protected, who need care, who need guidance. It's back to those unwanted identities.

But Jesus says, *I am the Good Shepherd.* In Jesus' vision for humanity, we can bring our whole selves—the fragile and weak parts of ourselves, alongside the powerful and strong parts of ourselves. In Jesus' vision for humanity, when we are sick, when we are exiled, when we are imprisoned, we don't become invisible or unwanted. The shepherd doesn't banish the weak, but he protects and guides and looks out especially for the weak, the forgotten, the sick. There's a lot to be said for sheep, for being humble enough to follow a shepherd.

Are you willing to be led by the shepherd? Or will you choose independence, destruction, toughness?

Will you permit yourself to be guided, cared for, protected? Or are you so invested in your identity as smart and strong and beholden to no one that you'll miss out on connection, and care?

DAY 53

Forgiveness

When I'm trying to forgive someone, I picture myself physically lifting that person off a big hook, like in a cartoon. I never want to. I prefer to stew and focus my anger on them like a laser pointer. I work on my anger toward them like I'm training for the Olympics, with tremendous dedication and force.

A friend of mine made me really mad, and my therapist suggested that really mad is always covering over hurt and fear, so if we're telling the whole truth here, she hurt me, and she made me feel scared and small and out of control. And that's worse than just making me mad. Every time I heard from her or about her, it hurt.

For a while, it brought me so much joy to be angry with her and to put her back up on the hook, over and over. I felt powerful, I think, like I could hurt her the way she hurt me. I exhausted myself imagining the same conversation again and again, but slightly different each time, saying clever things and finding loopholes in her lame arguments.

One night when I went over to a friend's house, she asked how I was doing. I told her that I had been having a hard time with my other friend lately. "Oh," she said. "When did you talk to her?" I rolled my eyes and puffed out my breath like I was a seventh-grade girl. "I, um, I actually didn't talk with her at all. I mean, it's been hard . . . in my head."

Gently, kindly, she paused, waiting for me to realize what I just said. "Hard in your head?" Again, gently, kindly. I had been spending hours in imaginary conversations, tying myself up in knots, planning out elaborate comebacks I should have actually said months ago.

I kept thinking about her, and the anger and the venom were starting to feel familiar. First, I thought about what happened. And then the muscles in my neck and back scrunched up, and I felt bad at the base of my skull. Even if lots of other parts of life were going well, there was this thing, this tightness in my shoulders and my neck. Then it got harder to breathe.

The thing that keeps me going with the anger is that I think I'm right. Why would I forgive someone who doesn't even think she needs to be forgiven?

This is why. Because I want my neck and my back muscles to stop hurting, to unfurl like window shades. Because she's not the only one on the hook. Because every time I hang her up on that hook, the hook reaches down and grabs me too.

When I told my friend that things had been hard in my head, I realized that I'm the only one suffering right now. My anger doesn't hurt the person at whom I am very angry, but it hurts me.

So I let her off the hook.

And I still have to keep letting her off, every day, sometimes several times a day. Not for her sake, but for mine, because I want off the hook. It's hard work, and I don't want to do it, but I keep doing it. I keep letting her off the hook, because when I do, I can breathe again.

How does forgiving someone else make you feel?

Mustard Seeds

Throughout the gospels, over and over Jesus compares the Kingdom of Heaven to the Kingdom of Earth, sort of like "the way it should or could be" versus "the way it is." The kingdom of God is the way of living and interacting and serving that every one of us aspires to—the kingdom way is the way of love, of justice, of peace, of mercy, of service. To be Christian is to always be pulling Heaven to Earth.

In an agrarian culture, using the image of the mustard seed and plant would have been like a shorthand, an easy shared understanding because of how familiar it is in their context.

Mustard shrubs grow very quickly—they want to grow, and they'll quickly take over any available soil, so they're used as ground cover to keep soil from eroding and to suppress soil disease. Mustard plants are able to leach toxic heavy metals like lead and cadmium from damaged soil and restore and heal the ground in which they're planted.

This isn't just a story about how a tiny seed makes a big plant, Jesus is talking about how a tiny seed that grows into a plant that spreads rapidly and heals everything around it, that keeps the soil from washing away, that kills disease, and that pulls the dangerous elements out of the soil to allow good things to grow.

This is what the kingdom of God is like: A plant that starts from almost nothing and heals and protects and restores as is grows. A plant that changes the very soil in which is planted.

As Christians, our lives should be increasingly shaped by this kingdom vision with each passing year. As we grow in Christlikeness, what we plant and harvest should be increasingly aligned with the kingdom.

That's not easy work, and none of us will get to a place where the circles overlap perfectly, but the way of Christ is to be moving with each passing month, each passing year to more and more of a kingdom legacy, instead of a legacy that centers only on ourselves, our own little kingdoms.

It's easy to think very small, to have a scarcity mentality that keeps us focused only on our own legacies—I'll just take care of my people, my corner, my little territory. When it feels sometimes like there's not enough to go around, it's easy to be driven by fear and selfishness, to assume that someone else will take care of everything else if we just focus very narrowly on our own needs. I get that.

But you don't need decades, and you don't need super-human capacities, and you don't need to get it all right every time, because the power of the kingdom can take something so small and grow something beyond our wildest imaginations. All we have to do is participate.

What choices are you making today that will be a kingdom legacy?

Needle and Thread

When Henry was born, we brought music into the delivery room that we thought would be the right sounds for him and for me, to serve as the soundtrack for his birth. We played songs by Ben Folds and Snow Patrol and Johnny Cash and the Beatles. Even now, when I listen to that playlist, it takes me back to that room, to the bright light in an otherwise dark room, to the tears running down my mom's face, and to Aaron's wide eyes, looking at once scared and amazed.

Just after Henry was born, and I mean *just* after—when the nurse, was weighing and measuring him, and his thin little gasping first cries sounded like the most beautiful sounds we had ever heard—at that moment, the only other thing we could hear, in the middle of the night in a silent hospital, was a song called "Needle and Thread" by Sleeping at Last. It's about God and angels and hospitals and love, and in that moment, it became ours—our song, Henry's song. Henry yelped and wiggled under the yellow light of the bassinet, and I laid in the bed motionless, spent and relieved and overwhelmed. I felt emptied in the best possible way, like I had done something brave and portentous, and now my work was done.

We heard the song again a few days later in our car when we brought Henry home from the hospital. Aaron was driving, and I was sitting in the backseat next to Henry in his car seat, my arms stretched over him, shielding him from any possible harm. I was also practicing Jedi mind tricks, willing all the other cars on the road to slow down and back away from our car. I imagined that everyone else on the road was either a bank robber in a getaway car or a drunk, and I glared at each one of them, preemptively rage-filled at their recklessness. And then that song began, and my rage and anxiety braided themselves into tense, muscular love. I cried all the way home, thinking about how God and his angels knitted this boy, our boy, together with needle and thread.

I know that the song isn't about Henry. I don't think it's about birth at all. Maybe it's about someone's uncle, or an episode of *Grey's Anatomy*. It doesn't matter, because the thing about a truly great song is that it becomes, truly and deeply, about our very own lives, regardless of what it started out as when it was written.

A few months later, Aaron and I went to a Sleeping at Last show, and when they played that song, we held hands, and I cried some more, and thought about our boy, about the night he was born, and the ride home, and the thousand moments in between—of life with Henry, and the rich and miraculous thing that it is to be his mother.

I wanted to tell the songwriter about it, about how thankful we were for his song, about how deeply his song traveled through the tenderest parts of our life, about how those words and sounds had become part of the story of one of the most sacred events of our lives. As I walked out to my car after the show, I almost went back to wait in line and tell him, but I knew that I would cry, not sweet little tears, but the kind that make your nose and eyeliner run, and that very possibly I would try to hug him, which would be mortifying for both of us. I don't know a lot about being a rock star, but I do know that just about the last thing a rock star wants, when there is a line of cute twenty-year-old girls in skinny jeans and black nail polish, is a thirty-year-old mom showing him pictures of her baby on her phone, trying to tell him something very personal and weepy about her son.

And so I didn't tell him, but if I had, this is what I would have said: Thank you. Thank you for creating something that speaks directly to my soul.

> When have you connected with art on a profoundly deep level? How have you let it change you?

Keep Going

Art slips past our brains straight into our bellies. It weaves itself into our thoughts and feelings and the open spaces in our souls, and it allows us to live more and say more and feel more. Great art says the things we wished someone would say out loud, the things we wish we could say out loud. My friend dances the way I would dance if I could. My other friend creates paintings that make me feel alive and free and like the world is more beautiful than it was before seeing them, and I'm better for having seen her paintings.

It matters, art does, so deeply. It's one of the noblest things, because it can make us better, and one of the scariest things, because it comes from such a deep place inside of us. There's nothing scarier than that moment when you sing the song for the very first time, for your roommate or your wife, or when you let someone see the painting, and there are a few very long silent moments when they haven't yet said what they think of it, and in those few moments, time stops and you quit painting, you quit singing forever, in your head, because it's so fearful and vulnerable, and then someone says, essentially, thank you and keep going, and your breath releases, and you take back everything you said in your head about never painting again, about never singing again, and at least for that moment, you feel like you did what you came to do, in a cosmic, very big sense.

I know that life is busy and hard, and that there's crushing pressure to just settle down and get a real job and khaki pants and a haircut. But don't. Please don't. Please keep believing that life can be better, brighter, broader, because of the art that you make. Please keep demonstrating the courage that it takes to swim upstream in a world that prefers putting away for retirement to putting pen to paper, that chooses practicality over poetry, that values you more for going to the gym than going to the deepest places in your soul. Please keep making art for people like me, people who need the magic and imagination and honesty of great art to make the day-to-day world a little more bearable.

And if, for whatever reason, you've stopped—stopped believing in your voice, stopped fighting to find the time—start today. Do something creative every day, even if you work in a cubicle, even if someone told you a long time ago that you're not an artist, or you can't sing, or you have nothing to say. Everyone has something to say. Everyone.

Because everyone, every person was made by God, in the image of God. If he is a creator, and in fact he is, then we are creators, and no one, not a bad seventh-grade English teacher or a harsh critic or jealous competitor, can take that away from you.

So to all the secret writers, late-night painters, would-be singers, lapsed and scared artists of every stripe, dig out your paintbrush, or your flute, or your dancing shoes. Pull out your camera or your computer or your pottery wheel. Today, tonight, after work or after the kids are in bed or when your homework is done, or instead of one more video game or episode, create something, anything, because it might be the most important thing you do. Keep going because we need it. I need it.

> What type of art brings you to life?

DAY 57

Honeysuckle Days

These are the honeysuckle days, where the air everywhere is heavy with that sweet floral smell. You walk into it, or the breeze brings it across the lawn on windy days, and it's like living for a minute inside a honey-scented cloud—almost too sweet, just shy of cloying. They say that in Victorian times the honeysuckle represented happiness, and it is, apparently, a Michigan thing, one I didn't know about. Michigan is known for cherries and blueberries and fudge and beer, and also, apparently, honeysuckle.

Late May and early June here smell like honeysuckle—we go for walks in the evening, and it grows along the dirt roads we like to walk down, a loop from the cottage out to Blue Star, taking unpaved roads there and back. A friend sent a care package, and a honeysuckle candle was in it, and without realizing it, I bought both dish soap and hand cream that are honeysuckle scented. A funny convergence, except that I always believe in paying attention to those funny convergences.

Honeysuckles are invasive—those happy sweet blooms strangle and smother other plants and they choke the trees they circle with their vines. That feels like something worth noting right now—that the sweet-smelling thing, the symbol of happiness is also deadly, a danger to other plants and trees.

And these clouds of sweet, honeyed air we're walking in are the result of a plant that destroys the plants around it. The honeysuckle overcomes them, uses them, breaks them. And so: privilege? Power? You can love that sweet-scented air, but you have to know that it exists because it choked the other plants. Sweet but dangerous. I don't want to be a honeysuckle—intoxicating but lethal. I want to be a plant that grows quietly, alongside, allowing for other plants to grow and thrive. And it's okay with me if the smell of this other plant I want to be is a subtler one: look where honeysuckle got us.

There is something about paying attention: when your world gets really small, you begin to realize how little you've been noticing up till that point. When you slow down, you notice more, I'm finding. You remember more. You are aware of everything.

Maybe that's why, against all odds, this feels like a creative time for me, because when the world gets really small, I'm able to focus in ways I can't when the world is big and loud and spinning. When everything's big and loud and spinning, I want to watch. I want to taste it all and see it all and feel it all. When things get silent and simple, I finally find something to say.

The Honeysuckle Days—when we read and cried and listened and prayed together on this green patch of land, seduced occasionally by that sweet cloud, but preferring, as we read and prayed, the cleaner, purer air, the air unperfumed by that sweet and dangerous vine.

In what quiet and small ways can you allow others around you to thrive?

A Well-Loved Sweater

I believe in a life of celebration. I believe that the world we wake up to every day is filled to the brim with deep, aching love, and also with hatred and sadness. And I know which one of those I want to win in the end. I want to celebrate in the face of despair, dance when all we see on the horizon is doom. I know that Death knocks at our doors and comes far too early for far too many of us, but when he comes for me, I want to be full-tilt, wide-open, caught in the very act of life. I think that's what we're here for, not for a passive, peaceful life, but to stand up in the face of all that lacks peace and demand more.

If I gave you a sweater, and you loved it, I would know because you would wear it so much, you'd be on the verge of wearing it out, because you loved it that much. It would be the sweater you wear on Christmas and to get coffee and that you sleep in sometimes and that you drag around in the back of your car and tie around your waist. It would start to smell like you, and it would get snags and get all stretched out, and just looking at it would make you tell a thousand stories of where it's been and who you've been in it.

That's what I want my life to be, like a well-loved gift. I

think life, just life, just breathing in and out, is a great gift. God gives us something amazing when he gives us life, and I want to live with gratitude. I want to live in a way that shows how much I appreciate the gift. If life were a sweater, I would wear it every day. I wouldn't save it or keep it for a special occasion. I would find every opportunity to wear that sweater, and I'd wear it proudly, shamelessly, for days on end.

> How can you live a life of gratitude?

DAY 59

The Divine Life

There's normal life, kind of day-to-day, make-breakfast, do-the-dishes kind of life, but just underneath that, like a throb of bass you feel in your chest, I feel a whole other thing going on. In the midst of taxes and email, there is something sacred, something special dipping and weaving, like a firefly, like a great song, and it reminds you that the dishes and the taxes are real, but so much more is real too. The sacred mixes in with the daily when you have a conversation with someone you love, or when you read a great book, or when you do something courageous. It's still just a normal day, but there's something bigger, something more compelling going on too.

One look at a baby's fingers and you just know that those little bundles of flesh and tiny bones are more sacred, more spiritual, than any thought or idea or theology could ever be. There are glimpses and whispers of the divine all through the daily, if we let ourselves look again, if we let ourselves believe that the world all around us is threaded through with divinity.

I live according to my faith when I love a meal that has been prepared carefully, when I notice texture and color and taste, when I let the flavor and scent of something fresh from the ground surprise me and bring me back to life. I demonstrate my theology when I dance all night with people I love, because this life is worth the best celebration we can offer up to it. I thank God every time I smell clean laundry and hear that little squeak of fingers on a guitar. For me, what God said when he made the world is a prayer: It is good. This world, it is good. The beauty of a perfect green apple is good. The first steps of a child are good. Watching my grandparents dance in their kitchen is good. It is good.

I have to remind myself that it is good. I have to create hope in my life, because there's something inside me that has radar for the bad parts of life. I walk into the kitchen and all I can see are crumbs on the counter, and I look in the mirror and I just see all the potential wrinkles forming. I have a dark, worst-case scenario sensor, and it takes over. It's all true. There are crumbs on the counter. I am definitely getting wrinkles. I just don't want to live in only that reality.

Because there is another reality. A better one. Hope and redemption and change are real, and they're happening all around me. So I choose to act out of that reality, because the other one makes life too hard. Life is painful, and we carry with us so much disappointment and heartbreak. But I'm fighting to save some space inside me where I can create hope. I can't live in the disappointment anymore. I've missed whole seasons of my life. I look back and all I remember is pain. I didn't love the gift of life because I was too busy being angry about the life I was given. I wanted it to be different. But being angry didn't change those things. It just wasted time. I can't take away the things that have happened to you or to me, but what we have, maybe as a reward for getting through all the other days, is today. Today is a gift. And if we have tomorrow, tomorrow will be gift.

What can you do to be more appreciative and intentional in your life?

Cold Tangerines

It's rebellious, in a way, to choose joy, to choose to dance, to choose to love your life. It's much easier and much more common to be miserable. But I choose to do what I can do to create hope, to celebrate life, and the act of celebrating connects me back to that life I love. We could just live our normal, day-to-day lives, saving all the good living up for someday, but I think today, just plain today, is worth it. I think it's our job, each of us, to live each day like it's a special occasion, because we've been given a gift. We get to live in this beautiful world. When I live purposefully and well, when I dance instead of sitting it out, when I let myself laugh hard, when I wear my favorite shoes on a regular Tuesday, that regular Tuesday is better.

Right now, around our house, all the leaves are falling, and there's no reason that they have to turn electric bright red before they fall, but they do, and I want to live like that. I want to say, "What can I do today that brings more beauty, more energy, more hope?" Because it seems like that's what God is saying to us, over and over. "What can I do today to remind you again how good this life is? You think the color of the sky is good now, wait till sunset. You think oranges